PRAISE FOR
When Bad Teams Happen to Good People

"Valerie Patrick takes all who want to run or be ⸻ ⸻ ⸻ ⸻ team but 'don't quite know the best formula to get there' on a comprehensive but utterly readable journey of personal anecdotes, practical tools, and commonsense advice. *When Bad Teams Happen to Good People* is a must-have for anyone intent on at least trying to understand the challenges and 'get it close to right.'"

—Nick Hamon PhD, CEO of IVCC
(Innovative Vector Control Consortium)

"*When Bad Teams Happen to Good People* acts as a comprehensive reference manual for all who seek team-based productivity and satisfaction, being an equally compelling read for team leaders, members, designers, and facilitators. Valarie Patrick provides practical, integrative guidance for proactively bettering oneself, assembling great teams, designing engaging meetings, fostering positive outcomes, and identifying and addressing team dysfunction when it inevitably arises. Dr. Patrick conveys proven, structured methods for team improvement, backed by science and illuminated by meaningful experiences drawn from her years of experience as a business leader and facilitator."

—Gary Fedder, PhD, Howard M. Wilkoff Professor of
Electrical and Computer Engineering at Carnegie Mellon University

"This book outlines tools to develop revised teamwork models that can accommodate challenges associated with fast-changing times."
—Dr. Devinder Mahajan, professor and graduate program director,
chemical and molecular engineering at Stony Brook University

"Valerie Patrick combines deep insight with practical guidance based on her years of executive leadership in the corporate world. In the crowded field of team effectiveness, Dr. Patrick offers clear-sighted direction on such key topics as facilitating team functioning, building high-performance teams, managing complex tasks, and strategic decision-making. A highly readable book to help you grasp what is needed for greater self-care and self-awareness in today's business context, while giving you the practical skills and tools needed to fix bad teams and design great ones. Highly recommended!"

—Chris Laszlo, PhD, professor of organizational behavior at Case Western Reserve University and author of *Quantum Leadership*

When
Bad Teams
Happen
to Good People

Your Complete Repair Guide
for Successful Teamwork

VALERIE PATRICK, PhD

Foreword by Anita Williams Woolley

This edition first published in 2021 by Career Press, an imprint of
Red Wheel/Weiser, LLC
With offices at:
65 Parker Street, Suite 7
Newburyport, MA 01950
www.careerpress.com
www.redwheelweiser.com

ISBN: 978-1-63265-182-2
Library of Congress Cataloging-in-Publication Data available upon request.

Cover design by Kathryn Sky-Peck
Cover illustration by TanyaJoy/iStock.com
Interior by Timm Bryson, em em design, LLC
Typeset in Adobe Garamond Pro

Printed in the United States of America
IBI
10 9 8 7 6 5 4 3 2 1

CONTENTS

Foreword by Anita Williams Woolley ix

Introduction: Why Do Bad Teams Happen to Good People? 1

Chapter 1: Bad Team? Heal Thyself First 11

Social Well-Being, 16

Personal Wellness Assessment (SPICE), 18

Physical Well-Being, 24

Intangible Well-Being, 29

Cognitive Well-Being, 33

Emotional Well-Being, 35

Chapter 2: Self-Awareness for the Will to Endure Bad Teams 41

Sense of Purpose and Teamwork, 44

Identity and Teamwork, 49

Personal Strengths and Teamwork, 58

Theory of Mind and Teamwork, 62

Chapter 3: Troubleshooting Team Leadership 67

Symptoms of Team Leadership Problems, 68

Types of Team Leadership Challenges, 71

Addressing Internal Leadership Challenges in Teams, 75

Addressing Team Member Needs, 86

Avoiding Team Leadership Thinking Traps, 92

Chapter 4: Troubleshooting Team Composition 97

Symptoms of Team Composition Problems, 99

The Challenges of Inclusion, 103

Leveraging the Diversity of Team Members, 110

Unshackling Team Members from External Influences, 114

Fixing Team Membership Problems, 120

Chapter 5: Troubleshooting Team Climate 127

Symptoms of Team Climate Problems, 128

Ways to Identify Team Climate Problems, 132

The Challenges of Team Creativity, 136

Leadership Dynamics Impacting Team Climate, 139

Team Member Role in Team Climate, 148

Chapter 6: Troubleshooting Team Operation 153

Types of Team Operations Problems, 155

Team Operation 101, 158

Operational Tactics to Support the Meeting Process, 165

Operational Tactics to Increase Team Member Participation, 175

Operational Tactics to Manage Disruption, 182

Chapter 7: Troubleshooting Meeting Design 187

Symptoms of Meeting Design Problems, 191

Principles of Good Meeting Design, 194

Components of Meeting Design, 198

Example of Advanced Meeting Design, 202

System for Mastering Meeting Design, 210

Endnotes 219

Index 237

FOREWORD

In every sector of our society, the need for teamwork is increasing because the complexity of the problems we face is increasing. And yet, as Valerie Patrick points out in the very first sentence of her book ". . . teamwork is hard." It's hard because so many of us lack the basic wiring, awareness, and behaviors to interact with others in ways that enable productive teamwork to take shape. But do not despair, because with this book in hand, you will be armed with information and practical tools to help you remedy some of these shortcomings and improve your team's work.

Because of my research on collective intelligence and my role in teaching the next generation of leaders how to manage their teams, I typically read any new book that promises to provide important insights on this topic. And I have to admit I am frequently disappointed by the lack of content in such books; often, there is really just one main idea, one nugget, that is expanded upon and elaborated with war stories for two hundred pages, and I'm left feeling like a short article in a business publication would have been sufficient to get the key points. Not so with this book—this book is literally jammed full of information, supported by research and accompanied by very practical tools and suggestions for concrete steps a leader could actually take to address the issues. As I read each chapter, I wrote down many notes and page numbers for sections I wanted to go back to and follow up on and think about how to integrate into my teaching. And as I read through the book, I would often think "Oh, this is my favorite chapter" but then I'd get to the next one, and I would like it just as much if not more! I particularly appreciated the material on designing and conducting meetings in chapters 6 and 7. So many of the core problems of team design and collaboration are on display in meetings; it's a place where so much time gets wasted in so many organizations, and yet very few leaders are ever educated on how to design and run them well.

There is a lot of wisdom throughout this book, and much of it goes well beyond just fixing teams. It will make you think about your purpose, look after your own well-being, and get acquainted with your personality, strengths, and weaknesses. These are insights that will be valuable in all areas of life, including teamwork. Time devoted to reading this book will be time well spent, and it's one you will want to keep to go back to and reference again and again.

—Anita Williams Woolley, associate professor
of organizational behavior and theory,
Tepper School of Business, Carnegie Mellon University

Why Do Bad Teams Happen to Good People?

Bad teams happen to good people because teamwork is hard. Can you imagine applying what you learned about social interactions from your family to the workplace? I grew up with three brothers, so my take would go something like this: Tim looks like he can punch hard, so I'm going to be nice to Tim and not say anything to provoke him. Jonathan is someone I can get to do work for me, and Matthew needs my guidance. Not only would it be unfair to judge Tim, Jonathan, and Matthew through the lens of my brothers, but it also would be unprofessional and ineffective to talk and behave according to these preconceptions. Teamwork is hard because social skills learned in one situation may or may not apply to another situation. In fact, research finds that 75 percent of workplace teams are dysfunctional because they fail to meet three or more of five measures of team performance.[1] So bad teams happen to good people because there are more bad teams than good teams in organizations.

Teamwork is harder today than at any other point in history because of the diversity of team members. For example, most workplaces have four to five generations of employees, which include the following: Traditionalists born before 1946, Baby Boomers born between 1946 and 1964, Generation X born between 1965 and 1976, Generation Y or Millennials born between 1977 and 1997, and Generation Z born after 1997. Each generation's values and beliefs are said to have been influenced by the salient events that occurred while they were growing up. The different generations of employees in the workplace also represent different age groups, so regardless whether a generation shares values and beliefs, perspective on work and life changes with age. For example, leaving a legacy becomes more important than material possessions as you age or after you have a near-death experience.[2] In addition to age and generation diversity, the US Census predicts there will be a minority majority or a white male minority by the year 2045. The trend toward a white male minority means increasing visible diversity in workplaces. This visible diversity brings different perspectives to the workplace and triggers nonconscious biases that can produce barriers to teamwork. Finally, there has been an explosion in the number of different majors that exist in colleges today compared to the past. For example, in 2020 Penn State offered about 275 different majors, whereas in 2015 it offered 160 different majors[3]—a 72 percent increase in five years! Interacting with siblings and school friends is easier than interacting with people who have different values, look different, and have a different major.

In addition to confronting age, visible, and expertise diversity across team members, teams are tackling more challenging problems. The output expected from teams today is more difficult than that expected in the past because more work is being done through teams today than in the past. Teams may handle many different challenges such as redesigning existing and creating new business processes, envisioning and designing new product and service concepts, doing customer satisfaction assessments, doing strategic planning, developing business and marketing plans, processing and acting on customer data, designing training programs, figuring out ways to reduce costs, troubleshooting manufacturing problems, implementing change programs, and handling product and service quality problems. In the past, some of today's team tasks could have and would have been handled by a manager or an executive. Today there is more context and input to consider than can be handled by any one person to tackle many of today's workplace tasks. In fact, organizations that have high financial performance ensure their teams "span the business and include diverse thinkers representing a range of skills."[4] A team's assignment is hard in and of itself and drives the need for diversity in team members, which confounds the difficulty of the work. Bad teams happen to good people because what we learn about working together outside the workplace does not prepare us for the innovation, problem-solving, and diversity challenges characteristic of workplace teams.

Teamwork in workplaces is the Olympics of social skills just like an a cappella group is the Olympics of singing. In an a cappella group, each singer needs to be at the peak of their singing craft for the group to perform well. Teamwork is the Olympics of social skills because team leaders and team members need to be at the peak of their collaboration craft to perform well with others.

A cappella singing may look easy, but there is an art and science to maintaining pitch, generating air support, creating resonance, singing in unity with others, and changing volume without musical accompaniment. There also is an art and science to engaging others, influencing them, operating creatively as a group, preparing for interactions, designing meetings, and facilitating meetings.

Proficient a cappella singers take care of themselves to perform their best singing in the group. For example, top a cappella singers hydrate themselves throughout the day, protect their voice from overexertion, and develop the muscles that support singing posture, air flow, sound initiation, and efficient breathing on demand. Similarly, the best collaborators take care of themselves to perform their best working with others as described in the first two chapters of this book. A cappella singers also learn and complete their responsibilities to the singing group. These singers are expected to learn and memorize their part, understand their part's role in each chord of the song, be able to hold their part against other parts, maintain pitch, sing accurate intervals, turn diphthongs with other singers, and execute an artistic plan. The best collaborators also learn and complete their responsibilities for working in a team as described in chapters 3 through 7 of this book.

Singers in an a cappella chorus learn about self-care routines and responsibilities from qualified others like singing coaches and accomplished singers. Similarly, collaborators learn about self-care routines and responsibilities for outstanding team performance from qualified others like teamwork trainers and trusted mentors. My purpose in writing this book is to use my teamwork experience (more than 10,000 hours of experience leading teams in a corporate environment and more than 10,000 hours of experience facilitating teams as a Certified Professional Facilitator) and scientific training (PhD in chemical engineering) to curate and annotate the science relevant to teamwork so others are empowered to improve team experiences. Chapters 1 and 2 provide evidence-based guidance on the types of self-care and self-awareness that can improve performance in team meetings. Chapters 3 through 7 provide tools and tactics to learn and complete the responsibilities of team members and team leaders.

It is an important time to expect more and get more out of teamwork whether or not you are part of a bad team because the problems organizations face are growing in complexity. Complex problems require new combinations of knowledge and strategies to address.[5] Teams are well suited to address complex problems because they provide a way to bring together different sources of knowledge and various strategic viewpoints. Of course, teams are well suited to tackle complex problems only when they are able to achieve high levels of performance as a group. But group performance can now be measured by collective intelligence, which is like intelligence quotient (IQ) except for a team.[6] Whether dealing with global pandemics, depletion of natural resources, or natural disasters exacerbated by climate change, teams need collective intelligence to help organizations navigate and thrive amidst complex challenges. This book shows team members and team leaders the self-care, self-awareness, and team tools needed to achieve collective intelligence.

An example of the impact of self-awareness on collective intelligence is the expectation you carry into a meeting. A past colleague of mine liked to say that a meeting is something where a lot go in but nothing comes out. An alternative view is that a meeting is an opportunity to experience the power of collaboration. Your expectation going into a meeting shapes your experience. If you view a meeting as something where a lot go in but nothing comes out, then you will not do your part to make that meeting successful. Further, a cynical attitude about meetings from one participant can spread to other participants, making it more likely for nothing of value to be accomplished. But if you view a meeting as an opportunity to experience the power of collaboration, then you will be looking for interactions that can produce change that matters. When you are not seeing an opportunity for change that matters, you will ask for clarity and explore what is possible. Your positive attitude will be contagious, and others will join in on the search for meaning and contribution. The ability of expectations and attitudes in a social setting to multiply is an example of the impact of self-awareness on human interaction. Such interaction can be magnified for good or for bad, and the choice is up to the people interacting. The leader of the people interacting may have a disproportionate influence on the outcome, but the people gathered also influence the outcome.

This book provides evidence for the importance of a quiet ego to unleashing team performance. A quiet ego is a state in which the "volume of the ego is turned down so that it might listen to others as well as the self in an effort to approach life more humanely and compassionately."[7] This holistic approach is based on balancing self-interests with the interests of others. Each chapter of the book highlights an aspect of the holistic approach demonstrated by a quiet ego. Chapter 1 describes how sources of well-being come from within the self and from others outside the self. Chapter 2 shows how knowing your identity in terms of values and personality helps decrease internal and external sources of psychological stress. Chapter 3 helps team leaders navigate the internal challenges associated with lack of skills and the external challenges associated with the behaviors of others. Chapter 4 shows that inclusivity requires you to balance what another person's negative emotion means to you and to the other person. Chapter 5 helps teams achieve equal participation across team members for creativity and problem solving, which requires both listening and speaking. Finally, chapters 6 and 7 help teams operate in strategic ways that benefit members and the people outside the team impacted by the team's work.

The ability to practice a quiet ego is a social skill because it takes into consideration the interests and inputs of others. Social skills, like all skills, fall on a continuum from meeting basic needs to mastery. An example of a simple social need on one end of the social skills spectrum is the need for friendship. Further along the social skills spectrum is the ability to make friends. A more advanced social skill than making friends would be networking to learn about new job opportunities or to learn new ways to reach career ambitions. Being able to accomplish challenging goals that require group thinking even when bad teams happen to good people is an example of an advanced social skill at the mastery end of the spectrum.

There are many different reasons to master teamwork. For example, you might be motivated by an envisioned benefit from improved teamwork skills. Benefits include increasing your contribution to an organization, getting your ideas noticed to advance your career ambitions, and increasing your networking opportunities by being recruited to more teams. Alternatively, you might be motivated by problems that can be avoided from improved teamwork skills. Improved teamwork skills can reduce sources of workplace stress, decrease the number of hours you work per week by spending less wasted time in meetings, and stop people problems with those different from you.

Social skill mastery for teamwork takes more than motivation to improve your teamwork skills and more than content from a teamwork expert like me. Skill mastery is also about what you do with the new content from the subject-matter expert. There are three ways to process content to master a new skill or subject area. One way is making connections to what you already know, which helps your brain figure out how to wire that new information for access when needed. A second way is deliberate practice,[8] which is the pursuit of perfect practice to make perfect. Imperfect practice leads to performance problems, and those problems drive insights to avoid those problems in the future and to inform the path to perfect practice. The third way to process content for skill mastery is building mental models that incorporate the wisdom gained from applying the skill to different situations. The better the mental model, the more that skill can be applied in different ways to address a variety of challenges.

Ways to process content are provided at the end of each chapter, but more or different work may be needed to fit your situation and needs better. For example, the first component of skill mastery—making connections between what you are learning and what you already know—can be accomplished in different ways. You can compare what you are learning to your existing beliefs and then formulate questions to address gaps and problems. Alternatively, you can reflect on past experiences that are consistent and inconsistent with what you are learning and then compare and contrast those experiences. Skill mastery means you have gained enough wisdom from practicing the skill to make the fine adjustments needed in different contexts.

I made progress on my journey to improve my teamwork skills by learning how to diagnose and address social problems in teams. You don't have to be born with good social skills to be able to improve your social skills. I score in the Asperger syndrome range on the autism-spectrum quotient, which predicts a tendency for poor social skills. However, I have been able to develop my teamwork skills to the point of supporting my career and life ambitions. Social problems are hard for the same reasons that math problems or other types of problems are hard: you haven't developed the insights and skills needed to tackle those hard problems—yet. This book is designed to help you along your journey to develop the insights and skills needed to tackle social problems in the context of teamwork.

Each workplace team I participated in had a designated team leader. Some teams rotate the role of leader, and some teams operate with a distributed leadership model. This book focuses on workplace teams with a designated team leader. It is just as dangerous to think that all is won with a talented leader as it is to think that all is lost with a poor one. While a team leader has a disproportionate influence on team operations and team climate, equal participation across the team leader and team members predicts high performance.[9] So leaders and members depend on each other to achieve the ultimate goal of high team performance regardless of the team leadership model.

Bad teams can be avoided at the outset when team leaders and team members embrace empowering expectations before agreeing to lead or participate in a team. For example, leaders need to understand the importance of the team to the organization's mission and what would happen if the team did not exist or did not achieve its mission. Members need a psychologically safe environment to ask questions and voice concerns about team goals to better understand how their thinking talents and expertise can be put to good use. Members also need to understand what type of input is expected from them well enough before a team meeting so they can be prepared to provide input at the meeting. Finally, members and leaders need motivation to commit to the success of the team both during and between meetings. A team is a system that operates within the bigger system of the organization. So leaders and members need to understand organizational influences on the team and the influences that the team has on the organization and on others in order to be successful. A team has a much better chance at being good if the leader and members are empowered to fully participate in meaningful ways.

Teamwork has taught me that wisdom is not possible without other people. The expertise I have developed in teamwork is thanks to the victims—I mean team members—of the early work teams I led all the way up to the teams of executives that I led late in my career. I tried to build on that expertise by incorporating the critical input of others in writing this book. This is a book about teamwork, so I must thank the virtual team of people who helped me improve this book with their valuable input (alphabetical by last name): Jean Bender, Leslie Billhymer, Grace Freedson, Joanne Gloisten, Bob Kumpf, Jill Meyers, Heather Patrick, George Pavlovich, Ken Picard, Jake Przybycien, Todd Przybycien, Cindy Sheffler, and Bill Shephard. A special shout-out to my first mentor who helped me find my passion for teamwork by assigning me to lead my first corporate team and whom the world lost in 2019: Mr. Tom King.

CHAPTER 1

Bad Team? Heal Thyself First

If you find yourself on a bad team, and you are not at your intellectual and emotional best, then chances are you will become part of the problem rather than part of the solution. I remember having a particularly challenging morning trying to entice my toddler son to get dressed and eat some breakfast so that I could take him to daycare and get to my staff meeting on time. I don't know whether he sensed my anxiety, but he was moving at what felt to me like a glacial pace. Of course, when we arrived at the daycare center, he was clingy and did not want me to leave him that morning—thank goodness for the caregiver who distracted him so I could duck out. I was late to the staff meeting, and the meeting leader made some snarky comment like, "Good of you to join us this morning." I wanted to say, "If you had to clothe, feed, and drag a reluctant two-year-old to daycare, then you would have been late to this early staff meeting too!" But that response would have made an already tense moment more tense. I couldn't think of anything positive to say, so thankfully I didn't say anything. In retrospect, I could have diffused the tense situation by saying something like, "If my two-year-old had a say in the matter, then I would not be here at all, but between you and me, I can't begin to tell you how excited I am to be in a room full of adults!"

You want to be at your intellectual and emotional best when you are part of a bad team experience so you can be part of the solution. Neuroscientists are uncovering the kinds of things that can be done to boost brain performance across different types of intelligences such as visual, verbal, logical, kinesthetic, musical, intrapersonal, interpersonal, and naturalistic.[1] This chapter summarizes key research findings on how to improve brain performance so that a good person can survive and even thrive in a bad team. It turns out that a healthy brain is the reward for practices that promote overall well-being. High brain performance helps you think in the moment in ways that are helpful to a bad team situation.

Research suggests that engaging in effective interactions may be more challenging than we realize. For example, a measure of social prowess is social intelligence, a concept that was first introduced in 1920 as a way to predict how well we can interact with other people.[2] But the idea of social intelligence has proven elusive enough that after one hundred years of ongoing research there is still no standard way to measure it.[3] In fact, archeologists have correlated the tripling in brain size for humans from 3.5 million years ago to today with changes in social structures that increased the number of daily interactions.[4] Interacting with other people is challenging enough that we had to evolve a three-fold bigger brain!

As you might surmise from my daycare story, this point in my career was hectic. I was assigned to be a member of a presentation team to impress potential buyers on the strengths of our business, which was up for sale. Then my all-time favorite boss was replaced by an older man who had been appointed to lead the research organization from the new company's European headquarters. Just when I had succeeded in building a good relationship with this new boss, he got promoted to a fantastic new opportunity in Asia. After only four months with the second man from the company's European headquarters appointed to lead the research organization,

I already sensed in my gut that he did not have adequate leadership skills. In fact, I was starting to question my decision to stay in the workforce with an adorable toddler at home.

One Friday afternoon, the leader I had doubts about called me into his office. I took a seat in front of his desk, and he got up to close his office door behind me. Before sitting back down, he got a very serious look on his face and said, "We need to talk. . . . You are spending far more money on books than anyone else in this research organization." What? Books? Our research organization was at risk of being dissolved because of a redundant organization at the new company's headquarters, and this numbskull was tracking book expenses! God forbid I be a learner to improve the performance of our research organization! I focused hard not to roll my eyes and not look incredulous as I listened to the boss's book rant. When he finished his rant, I forced a smile, thanked him for the input, and told him that I would correct the situation immediately. We shook hands, and I not only got out of his office as quickly as I could but also headed straight for my car and drove home early that Friday. The next day I felt pain in my right arm and told my husband that I thought I was having a heart attack. He called an ambulance, and I later learned that I had suffered a panic attack. A panic attack feels like a heart attack except that it dissipates as quickly as the onset once a medical professional confirms it is not a heart attack.

At that point in my career, I did not have the overall well-being needed to address the frustrations I had felt interacting with a boss who I believed had misplaced priorities. I could have offered great advice to the new boss based on the success of his predecessor to have helped him perform better. If I had channeled my frustration into the positive behavior of helping the new boss rather than the negative behavior of getting angry, then I could have improved my relationship with this boss. Instead, I internalized the frustrations of interacting with him, and my physical health suffered as a result. Thankfully, I left the research organization before it ended up being dismantled and its incompetent leader returned to a lower position in Europe.

Looking back, I remember a graduate student who was ahead of me at the California Institute of Technology (Caltech) and was married with three children. Can you imagine having a family and meeting the intellectual demands of pursuing a chemical engineering PhD degree at Caltech? Yet this student not only met the challenge but did so with flying colors. He routinely greeted me with a smile and reveled interacting with other graduate students. He also made time for daily exercise, practiced spiritual traditions with his family, and brought in a healthy lunch from home every day. I realize in retrospect that he knew something that I had not yet learned: you need overall well-being to be well with other people.

Several years later, a wise female pastor told me when I became a mother to a newborn son that I needed to take care of myself before I could take care of others. In talking to others, I found out that it's not that uncommon for first-time moms to become so focused on taking care of their newborn that they neglect to take care of themselves. The pastor could see how run-down I had become and that I needed some "me" time away from caring for the newborn to take care of my own needs. The pastor also reminded me that my needs weren't just physical like grooming, eating, exercising, and sleeping. There are also needs to be in the company of other adults and to do things to bring joy and inner peace. At the time, I was on family leave from my corporate job and was feeling guilty about looking forward to going back to work. However, by taking care of my well-being needs, I was able to enjoy both my work life and my home life.

Since my son was born, I have become a well-being nerd. I have been reading both popular science books and research articles about well-being for more than thirty years to support my leadership aspirations. Neuroscientists have found that different dimensions of well-being support brain functioning. In addition, they have found that social thinking activates many of the networks in our brain. Thus, building a healthier and better functioning brain improves social thinking and enables the development of social skills. For example, social prowess takes social well-being, cognitive well-being, and the ability to discern and follow social rules in the moment whether you are under any sort of stress. Furthermore, being able to discern and follow social rules under duress takes emotional, physical, and intangible well-being. These dimensions of well-being are needed to be at your intellectual and emotional best so you can be part of the solution when in a bad team.

You can remember the five dimensions of well-being by using the acronym SPICE: social, physical, intangible, cognitive, and emotional. The SPICE assessment in the next section will help you get a baseline of your current capacity to handle a bad team based on the five well-being dimensions.

The remainder of this chapter following the SPICE assessment provides evidence-based guidance on improving well-being in each of the five dimensions. I will share what the experts have to say and my own approach for each dimension as food for thought. Well-being, like sustainability, is a vector in which direction is more important than destination. The reason is that well-being is understood within the context of an individual's situation and life experiences just as sustainability is understood within the context of an organization's operations and customers. We can agree on ways to improve well-being or sustainability, but what well-being or sustainability looks like as a destination depends on several factors. Well-being for an individual depends on factors like age, genetic make-up, disease, personality, and resources. Sustainability for an organization depends on factors like the upstream supply chain, downstream supply chain, financial situation, political situation, and impact on social justice. Not only is direction more important than destination for well-being and sustainability, but thinking in systems is also an important factor. Well-being applies to the system of the human body while sustainability applies to the system of planet Earth. When you change an aspect of a system, that system will achieve a new state of balance that you want to be in a desirable direction. Balance is a guiding principle for the survival of all living things,[5] and neglecting this principle in improving well-being can lead to unhealthy outcomes. In other words, too much of a good thing can be bad for your well-being.

SOCIAL WELL-BEING

Neuroscientists are uncovering more and more about the importance of social well-being to our survival.[6] For example, social neuroscientists have discovered a network of regions in the brain that are activated during social interactions. In fact, scientists have found that our default mode of thinking is social, which means that we are wired to think socially as our best chance for survival. Furthermore, the higher our social well-being, the more likely we are to understand and resolve social problems getting in the way of team performance.

Neuroscientists have discovered that the brain's activation pattern in response to physical pain looks very similar to that in response to social pain, such as going through a divorce or having a frustrating team experience.[7] In fact, it is recommended that you take the same kind of medication that you would take for a headache when you need relief from an acute experience of social pain. Our brain evolved to treat social pain similar to physical pain in terms of the potential threat to our survival.

Social well-being has also been linked to physical health.[8] For example, a 2013 study found that the health risks from social isolation are comparable to those from cigarette smoking and high blood pressure. Social isolation in this study correlated most strongly with being unmarried, participating infrequently with religious activities, and lacking involvement in clubs or organizations.

If social isolation is linked to negative health outcomes, then it stands to reason that social engagement is linked to positive health outcomes. One networking expert claims that the most successful people tend to belong to seven different communities or groups on average.[9] Further, a psychology researcher found a correlation between the number of different social groups you belong to and your physical health.[10] This research study also concluded from a literature review that at least three strong social relationships are needed to be able to gain the health benefits associated with social well-being. Of course, you first need to make social connections before one or more of those connections can blossom into a strong relationship.

Social connections may be important to our very survival and health, but this doesn't mean that making such connections is easy. While connecting with another person is sometimes easy, social connection is still based on some fundamental skills. For example, building trust with another person starts with your ability to be trustworthy. How much are you going to trust a person who bad-mouths someone you know who is not present to defend themselves? Bad-mouthing others not present is an example of a behavior that is not trustworthy. Similarly, your ability to influence others depends on your ability to be influenced by others. Someone who will not acknowledge and try to understand your point of view on a topic is not going to be very good at influencing you to adopt their point of view on that topic. In other words, genuine social connection takes being socially considerate in how to interact with others.

Social well-being is produced by having an adequate number of strong, healthy relationships that provide joy in your life and that

PERSONAL WELLNESS ASSESSMENT (SPICE)

Social Well-Being

a. I'm an active member of ___ social groups as follows [list them]: _____
_____

    1. 1   2. 2   3. 3–6   4. 7   5. 8 or more

b. I have ___ friends that can bring me down or cause me emotional stress as follows [list them]: _____

    1. 3   2. 2   3. 1   4. zero   5. 4 or more

c. I have ___ friends that I can talk to about my troubles and can lift me up when I most need it as follows [list them]: _____
_____

    1. 1   2. 2   3. 3   4. 4–15   5. more than 15

d. I practice ___ of the following behaviors frequently or always [check all that apply].

___seek first to understand and then to be understood;

___maintain hopeful outlook on life;

___ when I disagree with another, I start by praising them for what I like and then provide constructive input on why I disagree;

___initiate conversation with someone who is withdrawn;

___start with trusting someone new until I can prove they can't be trusted.

    1. zero or 1   2. 2   3. 3   4. 4   5. all 5

e. I practice ___ of the following behaviors frequently or always [check all that apply].

___talk with complete honesty;

___demonstrate openness to different viewpoints and people;

___am completely transparent with my point of view;

___own up to my mistakes;

___am loyal to a friend not present;

___take initiative to change things for the better;

___listen to understand another's viewpoint;

___build strong character in others.

    1. 2 or less   2. 3   3. 4–5   4. 6–7   5. all 8

are comparable to those from cigarette smoking and high blood pressure. Social isolation in this study correlated most strongly with being unmarried, participating infrequently with religious activities, and lacking involvement in clubs or organizations.

If social isolation is linked to negative health outcomes, then it stands to reason that social engagement is linked to positive health outcomes. One networking expert claims that the most successful people tend to belong to seven different communities or groups on average.[9] Further, a psychology researcher found a correlation between the number of different social groups you belong to and your physical health.[10] This research study also concluded from a literature review that at least three strong social relationships are needed to be able to gain the health benefits associated with social well-being. Of course, you first need to make social connections before one or more of those connections can blossom into a strong relationship.

Social connections may be important to our very survival and health, but this doesn't mean that making such connections is easy. While connecting with another person is sometimes easy, social connection is still based on some fundamental skills. For example, building trust with another person starts with your ability to be trustworthy. How much are you going to trust a person who bad-mouths someone you know who is not present to defend themselves? Bad-mouthing others not present is an example of a behavior that is not trustworthy. Similarly, your ability to influence others depends on your ability to be influenced by others. Someone who will not acknowledge and try to understand your point of view on a topic is not going to be very good at influencing you to adopt their point of view on that topic. In other words, genuine social connection takes being socially considerate in how to interact with others.

Social well-being is produced by having an adequate number of strong, healthy relationships that provide joy in your life and that

m. I currently engage regularly in ___ activities that inspire me to be a better person and see the good in the world as follows [list them]: _____

_____

   1. none   2. 1   3. 2–4   4. 5–10   5. 11 or more

n. Which one of the following phrases most closely describes you?

1. I can't tell what others are thinking.
2. I can sometimes tell what others are thinking and feeling.
3. I try to cheer up a person who appears sad or lonely.
4. While I have a good sense of what others are feeling and thinking, I always mirror my sense to them to confirm whether or not I'm right before doing anything else.
5. I can tell what the people I know well are thinking or feeling, and I act accordingly.

o. Which one of the following phrases most closely describes you?

1. I can't stop myself from jumping to conclusions about what another person says when it is antagonistic or upsetting to me.
2. I spend more time thinking about what others think of me than about what I think of myself.
3. Interpreting the behaviors of others helps me respond in a social situation.
4. I am often able to stop or control a bad reaction to another person so I can think before I act.
5. I don't have uncontrolled reactions toward other people.

Cognitive Well-Being

p. I completed brain teasers on ___ of the last 7 days.

   1. none   2. 1   3. 2–3   4. 4–6   5. 7

q. I engaged in an activity that tapped into my creativity (i.e., brainstorming, drawing, making music, composing, writing, and so on) on ___ of the last 7 days.

   1. none   2. 1   3. 2–3   4. 4–6   5. 7

Physical Well-Being

f. I drink ___ ounces of water a day on average.

   1. no idea   2. 16–32   3. 33–63   4. 64–84   5. 85 or more

g. I consume ___ grams of added sugar (sugar beyond what occurs naturally in fruits and vegetables and in all forms including honey, confectionary, granulated, and high fructose corn syrup) a day on average.

   1. no idea   2. 50–69   3. 21–49   4. 0–20   5. more than 70

h. I get ___ minutes of aerobic exercise a week on average.

   1. no idea   2. 0–60   3. 61–89   4. 90–200   5. more than 200

i. My strength-training activities can best be described as:

1. none
2. Occasional sit-ups and push-ups
3. 1 to 2 times a week with resistance
4. 3 to 5 times a week, mix of weight machines and free weights
5. daily with free weights

j. I got ___ hours of sleep the last three nights.

   1. < 15   2. 15–20   3. 21–24   4. 25–40   5. > 40

Intangible Well-Being

k. Which phrase best resonates with you?

1. It's a cruel world and being cynical allows you to get some entertainment out of it.
2. Stay true to yourself at all costs.
3. Help out others when you can.
4. I've got to take care of myself so I can be there for others.
5. True fulfillment comes from sacrificing yourself for others.

l. I currently engage regularly in ___ spiritual practices as follows [list them]: _____

   1. none   2. 1   3. 2–4   4. 5–10   5. 11 or more

PERSONAL WELLNESS ASSESSMENT (SPICE) *continued*

You can use the following table to score your assessment by filling in the numbers of your answers and summing each column. The key for the score in a given well-being dimension is a guide for an average adult living in the United States with no chronic or acute illnesses. The next section summarizes the latest research findings on social well-being.

Social Well-Being	Physical Well-Being	Intangible Well-Being	Cognitive Well-Being	Emotional Well-Being
a. _____	f. _____	k. _____	p. _____	u. _____
b. _____	g. _____	l. _____	q. _____	v. _____
c. _____	h. _____	m. _____	r. _____	w. _____
d. _____	i. _____	n. _____	s. _____	x. _____
e. _____	j. _____	o. _____	t. _____	y. _____
Total: _____	Total: _____	Total: _____	Total: _____	Total: _____

5–9: Uh Oh;   10–14: Room for Improvement;   15–19: Doing Good;
20–22: Doing Great;   23–25: May Be Overdoing It

you can turn to when times are tough. Is there consensus on how many strong, healthy relationships are needed to derive the health benefits associated with social well-being? The number depends on your personal preference. For example, my husband has always preferred a small circle of close friends, whereas my circle of close friends is a little larger. Some of my friends have even larger circles of close friends. Social science does provide some guidelines. The minimum is three, and the maximum is fifteen strong healthy relationships with people we care deeply about.[11] You know you have a healthy relationship when the other person energizes you, brings you joy, and lifts you up when you are down or in a funk. Another person will energize you, bring you joy, and lift you up because you do the same for them—healthy relationships are reciprocal.

Social science provides some guidance for the behaviors that help you develop strong and healthy relationships with your friends and family members. These behaviors include the following:

- listening to be able to explain the other person's viewpoint,
- communicating with no hidden agendas and with thoughtful honesty,
- talking about your feelings in response to a situation that may be minor now but could be damaging to the relationship in the longer term,
- being hopeful in interactions when the other person is feeling down,
- seeking to understand what another person is feeling,
- taking your share of the responsibility for things that go wrong in a relationship,
- trusting that the other person has your best interests in mind until you can prove otherwise, and
- having an objective view of your skills and accomplishments so you are not bragging or fishing for compliments.[12]

Even the US Army recognizes the importance of the things an individual needs to do to promote healthy relationships with their tips for a person to develop what they call "social fitness."[13]

Keep in mind that there is a difference between popularity and social well-being. Popularity is typically based on a person's fashionable appearance, high energy, friendly face, and high confidence. In contrast, social well-being is based on deep relationships, which take time to build. This kind of relationship comes from discovering things you like to do together, talk about, dream about, set goals about, and support each other about. It is social well-being that leads to health benefits, not popularity. To build your social well-being, be yourself and develop close relationships with the three to fifteen people who understand you and like spending time with you. The lack of social well-being has been correlated with bad health outcomes, but there are other routes to bad health outcomes.

PHYSICAL WELL-BEING

In my college days, one student would sit on one side of the college cafeteria and absolutely stuff his face full of food. Then he would disappear for about twenty minutes or so. Seemingly out of nowhere, he would reappear on the opposite side of the cafeteria, again stuffing his face full of food. He repeated this pattern two to four times at every meal. One of my friends said that he was bulimic, which I had to ask her to explain—this was before the Internet was open to the public. Bulimia is an eating disorder that uses binge-purge cycles to manage weight; it is unhealthy in addition to being unappealing. While I could understand the binging because the food at the college was amazing—all prepared fresh by local Amish women—I could not understand the punishment of purging. It turns out that people who suffer from eating disorders have become victims to shame and self-hate. In so doing, people with eating disorders cross the line from normal dieting to health and emotional problems.

At our college, we had the "freshman twenty" rather than the more typical "freshman ten"—the weight you gain being on a college meal plan your freshman year. After gaining my freshman twenty, I got active my sophomore year with a regular dance class, lots of racquetball, running, and regular visits to the weight room. I also paid more attention to what I was eating. What was surprising to me was how much more upbeat I felt, how much more clear my thinking was, and how much more energy I had as a result of starting a physical exercise program in college. I also lost weight, but the impact on my mood, energy, and thinking far outweighed the impact on my weight (pun not intended). An improved mood, higher energy, and increased clarity of thinking also help performing in teams.

There is a big body of literature surrounding both diet and exercise. However, caution is needed when approaching the literature because weight loss and fitness are two big businesses in the United States. Revenues from US health and fitness clubs in 2018 totaled $32 billion,[14] while revenues from weight-loss products and services totaled $72 billion.[15] In fact, the weight-loss and fitness industries combined were about one-third the size of the apparel industry in 2018.[16] In this section, I've taken care to focus on scientific articles that are peer-reviewed and based on sound scientific processes and to avoid public articles lacking scientific substance.

While in graduate school I was trained as an aerobics instructor to learn how to keep aerobics students safe both during and following strenuous aerobic exercise. I also learned about fitness fashion. The understanding of the impacts of aerobic exercise on the body today is much more sophisticated than it was back then. For example, scientists now understand that aerobic exercise can change the heart's structure and function and also the volume of blood vessels.[17] Scientists also better understand how aerobic exercise improves lung function.[18] Neuroscientists have also gotten into the picture and have shown correlations between exercise and improved cognitive function.[19] There is also evidence that aerobic exercise improves resilience to stress such as that caused by social interactions.[20] So aerobic exercise has direct correlations with reducing stress and improving the performance of many bodily organs, including the heart, lungs, and brain.

A good complement to aerobic exercise is strength training. For example, weight training has been shown to improve bone mass density, muscle strength, and balance, which help prevent you from getting injured when doing aerobic exercise.[21] Weight training also helps combat the decrease in resting metabolic rate (the rate at which your body burns calories at rest) that occurs with aging.[22] A decreasing metabolic rate can lead to weight gain if eating habits are not adjusted to compensate for the fewer calories being burned. Thus, weight training helps you maintain a healthy weight as you age and helps keep you safe from injury when doing aerobic exercise to improve heart, lung, and brain function.

Aerobic exercise is sustained physical activity keeping your heart rate at a target level that depends on your age and level of fitness. You can calculate your target heart rate for aerobic exercise from your age and resting heart rate.[23] You can also measure your heart rate while exercising to make sure you get in the target heart rate zone and stay in that zone for the maximum physical and cognitive benefits from that exercise.[24] For example, doing fifteen minutes of sustained aerobic exercise at least three times a week has been shown to decrease the risk for dementia and Alzheimer's later in life regardless of when you start.

To maximize health and cognitive benefits, choose aerobic exercises that you can enjoy and commit to and that won't put too much stress on the body. You have probably heard of runners getting shin splints, which are the pains in the front of the lower legs believed to be caused by too much stress on the tissue connecting the muscle to the shin bone.[25] Shin splints are caused when the cushioning and support from your exercise shoes are insufficient for the type of surface you are exercising on relative to the force of impact from the exercise. When you exercise, you should take into account the best shoes for your body to absorb the impact from the exercise without damage and the safest equipment for the exercise. You can do aerobic exercise at home, in a fitness club, in an exercise class, or outside; there are many options. Don't forget to stretch the muscles that you will be using in the aerobic exercise before and after exercise to minimize muscular fatigue and damage.

Weight training is using resistance from gravity and weights to increase muscle mass and help prevent injury during aerobic exercise. If you have never done weight training before, then you might want to learn the proper use of weights and equipment to increase muscle mass and prevent injury during aerobic exercise. Proper use will help keep you safe from injury during weight training. You can hire a fitness trainer or find online content that comes from a qualified health professional or fitness trainer to learn how to do safe and effective strength training.

The next component of physical well-being in addition to exercise is diet. From my research and experience with many different approaches to healthy eating over the years (over five decades, but who's counting), I have come up with the following five principles for my physical well-being from diet:

- Drink at least 64 ounces of fluids a day.
- Consume less than 20 grams of added sugar a day (the natural sugar found in foods does not count).
- Minimize or eliminate the consumption of artificial sweeteners (including high-fructose corn syrup) and saturated fats.

- Consume eight to fifteen half-cup servings of fruits and vegetables every day.
- Decrease consumption of red meat relative to fish, chicken, turkey, pork, and plant-based proteins.

Following these five principles for a healthy diet has helped me maintain cognitive acuity and high energy throughout the work day and beyond.

The final component to physical well-being, in addition to diet and exercise, is sleep. Neuroscientists now understand that sleep is important to learning and memory.[26] Furthermore, a system for removing waste products from the brain, called the glymphatic system, has been discovered; it operates while you sleep.[27] The glymphatic system operates similar to the lymphatic system in the body except that it uses glia cells in the human brain, whereas the lymphatic system uses lymph nodes throughout the body. The glymphatic system removes dangerous toxins from the brain that naturally accumulate from the brain's operations during the day and that have been linked to neurodegenerative diseases like Alzheimer's.[28] While scientists agree there is more to understand about why the body needs sleep, the cognitive and health benefits are reason enough to get adequate and productive sleep.

The question remains on how much sleep is needed and what productive sleep looks like. The National Sleep Foundation has made a recommendation for the average range of sleep needed by a healthy person based on their age.[29] For example, newborns need between fourteen and seventeen hours of sleep, and adults need between seven and nine hours of sleep. An adult can still be healthy with sleep outside of the recommended range; however, being healthy with a sleep amount significantly outside the range is rare. The National Sleep Foundation also has identified what healthy sleep patterns look like based on their research,[30] and it has described the conditions for high-quality sleep.[31] You know you had a good night's sleep if you fell asleep within thirty minutes, you didn't wake up for more than five minutes, you didn't wake up more than once for up to twenty minutes, and you were asleep for at least 85 percent of the time in bed. I probably should have addressed sleep quality at the beginning of the book so you won't fall asleep while reading this because of a poor night's sleep.

Physical well-being will depend on what you eat, how you exercise, and your sleep habits. I have noticed a correlation between my physical well-being and my intellectual capabilities. For example, when I get a good night's sleep, do aerobic exercise and weight training early in the day, and eat well, my abilities to be creative, solve problems, and think clearly are enhanced. We can agree that seven to nine hours of sleep is a good target based on the study by the National Sleep Foundation. We can also agree that doing fifteen minutes of sustained aerobic exercise at least three times a week will boost cognitive functioning into old age. Beyond that, it is up to you to develop healthy eating and exercise habits that work for your preferences and lifestyle. Just as there are tangible things you can do to enhance physical well-being, there are tangible things you can do to improve intangible well-being.

INTANGIBLE WELL-BEING

My first attempt at singing a solo in my life happened to be as an adult in my church. I had rehearsed the solo over and over again with the piano accompanist. When it came time to perform, the accompanist gave me a reassuring nod before beginning to play. When it came time for me to start singing, I could feel my arms and legs trembling and hear the trembling replicated in my voice. I remember looking down for a brief moment and asking for God's help to calm my nerves—I was in a church after all. Then, like magic, the trembling in my body stopped, and my voice became more solid and pleasant for the congregation to hear. I remember feeling grateful that God had come to my rescue to enable me to sing. I didn't even mind when one of the older ladies in the back of the church said, "Your solo was nice, but I like it better when you sing with the choir." It wasn't until later that I would learn that nervousness produces shallow breathing, which, in turn, causes the singing voice to waver. With experience, I would also learn that the supportive faces of listeners help fuel confidence and decrease nervousness. But I don't think I could have gotten through that first terrifying experience of singing a solo without calling on the help of something beyond my conscious self.

Intangible well-being can be thought of as the ability to manage nonconscious brain processes when those processes do not serve us well in a given situation. For example, when I started to sing my first solo, my nonconscious brain could have brought up a stored memory of my first flute solo, which did not go very well and would have produced doubts in my ability to perform. Neuroscientists understand that the brain is driven to automate as many tasks and processes as possible to conserve energy because it consumes more energy than any other organ in the body.[32] The brain doesn't want to use energy when it doesn't have to, and automated tasks consume less energy than tasks that require focus and conscious thinking. To automate tasks, the brain searches for stored experiences that are related to what we are doing and then pieces together a program for us to complete the task on auto-pilot. This process happens automatically and very rapidly in our nonconscious brain, so we are not even aware it is going on. However, by thinking about what is going on in the present moment, we can switch off this automatic processing and focus on doing the task well in the given moment. My thinking was brought into the present moment during my solo when I noticed my physical shaking and asked for God's help to calm my nerves.

Lots of different people offer explanations of how to develop intangible well-being and what it should feel like. Some people believe that intangible well-being is possible only if you are devoted to practicing an organized religion. But long before there were formal religions, people used storytelling as a vehicle to think about others and about beings beyond the self.[33] Still other people are prescriptive about the types of practices needed to truly experience intangible well-being. This type of well-being can be accessed in many different ways, as evidenced by the many different formal and informal spiritual practices that have originated from the traditions of the East, the West, Christianity, Judaism, Buddhism, Sufism, Zen, Chassidism, Hinduism, Native Americans, Africans, atheists, secular humanists, and other sources. However, scientists are showing that you can experience intangible well-being whether or not you practice a religion and that different practices help develop it.

One way to develop intangible well-being according to science is to nurture self-transcendent positive emotions (STPEs) as a way to build resilience to life's distresses and moments of adversity.[34] STPEs are elicited by experiencing a display of physical beauty or displays of talent and moral beauty by others that inspire you to become a better person. For example, the positive emotions I feel when I watch a spectacular sunset on the edge of Lake Champlain in northern Vermont are STPEs. STPEs were found to inspire people to behave better toward others because the experience of STPEs correlated with perceiving others and the world as more well meaning and with a belief that life is meaningful. You will be more resilient to adversity and distress when you see life as meaningful and you can see the good in others and the world. You can experiment with the types of volunteer work, experiences, animals, movies, books, and other content that trigger STPEs for you.

Another way to develop intangible well-being is through spiritual practices. Neuroscientists have found a connection between oxytocin, a neurotransmitter associated with feelings of pleasure and reward, and spirituality.[35] Spirituality is the belief that your life has meaning within the context of being connected to something bigger than yourself. A spiritual practice helps you connect with something bigger than yourself, such as a family, community, or divine being. For example, one of my spiritual practices is writing down three things that I am grateful for at the end of every day and why I am grateful for those things. Invariably, I learn that the things I am grateful for are those that contribute in some positive way to the lives of other people. There are many different spiritual practices to choose from and explore to find what is most helpful for you to connect with your inner propensity to do good for others.[36] Be open to changing your spiritual practices over the course of your life because their impact on filling you or draining you of positive energy may change as your life evolves. On balance, you want to end up with a surplus of positive energy from your combined spiritual practices to become resilient to adversity and stress.

A final example to develop intangible well-being is through mindfulness meditation. This practice has been shown to improve self-control and the ability to focus, which are both needed to override the nonconscious brain when needed.[37] In fact, mindfulness programs have been shown to improve management of chronic pain, prevent depression relapses, and improve substance-abuse outcomes.[38]

Intangible well-being is your source of inspiration to realize life's opportunities and your source of resilience to life's challenges and misfortunes, such as bad teams. You can learn more about the different formal religions practiced around the world and in different communities to see if something resonates there for you. You can also discover the spiritual practices used by different people to home in on what might support your intangible well-being. Remember to be open to the possibility that what you need for intangible well-being may change over the course of your life, and the same can also be said for cognitive well-being.

COGNITIVE WELL-BEING

I figured out that I was in a different math class than my grade-school friends when several of them were talking about their math homework and it was quite different from mine. When I asked my mom about it, she said that my math skills were not as well developed as those of my friends. It became my mission to change this situation because I wanted to be in the same math class with my friends. I would end up earning degrees in engineering, so mathematics became one of my strengths!

Neuroscientists believe that the creation of new neurons in the brain is important to learning and memory.[39] They now understand that our brains have the capacity to grow new neurons and make new neural connections in our brains throughout our lifetime.[40] There is also growing consensus among scientists that each different kind of thinking involves many different regions of the brain working together in a network rather than an isolated region.[41] In fact, your ability to learn as measured by IQ is a necessary but insufficient condition for social intelligence. Cognitive well-being means ensuring the ability to think and learn throughout your life, which produces new neurons in the hippocampus and changes neural connections in your brain.

Research seems to support the "use it or lose it" philosophy for keeping your brain healthy. While the scientific evidence is still sparse, there is some support that the act of learning leads to the production of new neurons.[42] That's right—learning begets learning! This finding is thrilling to me as a person who loves to learn but may not be so interesting to others. In addition, specific types of training can increase intelligence.[43]

Evidence suggests that cognitive capacity is a key component of creativity. For example, some specific strategies for learning enhance your creativity.[44] In addition, creativity is believed to involve many brain regions important to critical thinking, including the imagination, executive attention, and salience networks.[45] The imagination network, also known as the default mode network, is involved with personal meaning making, mental simulation, and perspective taking. The executive attention network is involved with concentrating on a challenging lecture or engaging in complex problem solving and reasoning that puts heavy demands on working memory. Finally, the salience network is involved with motivation. In addition, cognitive psychologist Dr. Scott Barry Kaufman says: "A connection to our inner selves and our stream of consciousness is undeniably what makes us creative."[46] So creativity is not just about accessing the networks in the cortex or conscious brain but also about accessing nonconscious brain networks. In other words, creativity takes some serious thinking and whole brain work!

Of course, the acts of learning and creativity are not enough to keep your thinking in top shape. There is scientific evidence for additional factors needed to keep your thinking healthy. Specifically, getting regular aerobic exercise, getting adequate sleep, effectively managing stress, and studying or listening to music are important to good brain functioning.[47]

Finally, there is evidence that good nutrition is important to cognitive health.[48] This finding is not surprising because good nutrition is important to physical health and your brain controls all the operations in your body. In fact, some foods may be particularly important to cognitive health, such as blueberries, salmon, avocados, and dark chocolate.

For the sake of cognitive well-being, get curious so you can find new topics to learn about at every point of your life, especially once you are out of school. There are also many different ways to boost your creativity for cognitive well-being that you can explore.[49] One technique that improved my creativity was personal brainstorming in which I would articulate a personal problem such as "how to have an engaging family vacation" and then generate ideas for twenty minutes. Finally, practicing physical well-being will also benefit your cognitive well-being. It turns out that emotional well-being improves critical thinking in social situations like teams.

EMOTIONAL WELL-BEING

I was in a meeting called by the director of research (DR) with a respected senior science fellow (SSF) near the top rung of the scientific career ladder at the company. The SSF was a brilliant and kind man who had helped me with technical problem solving more than I care to admit. The DR was new to the organization and had taken me under his wing as my mentor and sponsor. The purpose of the meeting was for the DR to assign me as a liaison between the SSF and a business executive. But as the DR opened the meeting with an explanation of the meeting purpose, the SSF interrupted with a behavior and attitude I had never seen from him before. The SSF moved forward in his chair toward the DR and accused the DR of wanting to get rid of him because his intelligence was a threat to the DR. The DR's fair face then turned the same color as his red hair, and he bellowed a response from a standing position that the SSF would do whatever he told the SSF to do. The physical posturing and verbal abuse of these two escalated from there with their faces getting closer, their voices getting louder, and their language getting fouler. I was frozen in shock and maybe even in fear. I am usually good with managing conflict in team meetings, but I could not think of anything to say in this situation. Eventually, the DR ordered the SSF to leave the room, and I quickly excused myself for needing to get to another meeting but really I just wanted to get out of there too.

There are many examples of how emotions can take control of our thinking and behavior. The brain's emotion systems are part of our nonconscious brain. A whole host of feelings can result from the brain's negative emotion systems, including fear, nervousness, hostility, anger, disgust, guilt, shame, self-loathing, sadness, boredom, and loneliness. When our negative feelings run amuck or get ahead of our rational thinking, we can do and say things that we later regret. It can be helpful to learn your body's early signals that a negative emotion system has been triggered. The next time you experience strong negative feelings like fear, hurt, or anger, pay attention to what happens to your body. Pay attention to physical cues like furrowing your brow, tensing your shoulders, getting a dry mouth, being short of breath, or feeling a tightening in your stomach. Also pay attention to behavioral cues like raising your voice, pointing your finger, crossing your arms, becoming very quiet or withdrawn, or making noise with objects like a door or your desktop.[50] The sooner you can recognize when a negative emotion system has been activated in the nonconscious brain, the better able you are to pause and think before speaking or acting from a place of high negative emotion, which is an example of emotional intelligence.

Scientists define emotional intelligence in terms of what it takes to lead a successful life according to the following four dimensions:[51]

- Perceiving emotions: knowing one's own emotions or becoming aware of a feeling as it is happening and recognizing the emotions of others

- Using emotions: motivating oneself and channeling or controlling emotions to enable and optimize performance
- Understanding emotions: being able to label emotions and distinguish between related emotions of yourself and others as well as having insight into how different emotions are related
- Managing emotions: managing your emotions and those of others you are interacting with in a way that creates the desired interaction and outcome

Emotional well-being comes from having emotional intelligence. There has been some consensus among scientists on how to measure emotional intelligence, unlike social intelligence, depending on the need and intended use of the assessment.[52]

The brain's emotion systems are triggered primarily by our interaction with others. You can probably think of at least a few examples of how the behaviors of others in the workplace have triggered your emotion systems. For example, one day my boss called to tell me that I had been demoted as a result of a reorganization and the new lower position and reduced salary would take effect in thirty days—what a joyful day that was! While emotions originate in the nonconscious part of the brain, emotions become conscious when we become aware of the feeling triggered by the brain's emotion system.

Specific regions and chemistries in the brain for seven different emotion systems have been identified.[53] Four of these seven emotion systems are called "rewarding" because they point out things that support our survival. The remaining three systems are called "aversive" because they point out things that threaten our survival. If these emotion systems are functioning properly in the brain, then our rewarding systems tell us what situations and people to engage, and our aversive systems tell us what situations and people to be cautious of or to avoid. The caveat is that biology biases the threat system over the reward system. Our brain dedicates five times more real estate to the threat system than to the reward system, and the threat response is stronger, longer lasting, and more common than the reward response.[54]

While our brain's emotion systems are important to our survival and functioning, we can get pretty freaked out by others expressing feelings in the workplace. In my experience, men and women are both especially concerned when women express feelings in the workplace. Why are we so worried about expressing feelings in the workplace when emotion systems are so important to our well-being? The answer comes from social psychology.[55]

Every culture has expectations of what behavior is appropriate for a man versus a woman when it comes to feelings. In the United States, men are expected to exercise control over feelings, be rational, and use feelings to enhance performance. Women are expected to understand their own feelings and the feelings of others, talk about feelings, be empathetic, and care for others. Because the US workforce consisted mostly of men until 1964, when the Civil Rights Act was passed, it is not surprising that the expression of feeling other than in support of performance is still uncommon in workplaces. Even today, the upper echelons of US organizations are still predominantly men.[56] Interestingly, understanding and navigating the gendered norms for feelings in the workplace are aspects of emotional intelligence often not addressed. The idea of gendered norms for feelings adds the following aspect of emotional intelligence: how to factor in gendered norms for feelings in getting desired outcomes. Navigating gender diversity beyond emotional intelligence is addressed in chapter 4, "Troubleshooting Team Composition."

Emotions are our friends: emotions on the negative spectrum help us survive, and emotions on the positive spectrum help us thrive. In managing your own emotions and those expressed by others, the journey toward emotional well-being takes situational response to the brain's emotion systems. A situational response to emotion is expressing feelings and behaving in ways appropriate to the situation and to the desired outcomes.

This chapter showed that social prowess develops from a healthy social life, being smart, and being able to behave appropriately to a social situation such as a team regardless of your current frame of mind. The ability to behave well in social situations regardless of your frame of mind takes developing emotional intelligence, physical health, and intangible well-being. You can remember the key dimensions of social prowess with the acronym SPICE for social, physical, intangible, cognitive, and emotional well-being. The more you SPICE up your life, the more you will develop the social prowess needed to handle bad teams. In the next chapter you will learn the role of self-awareness in improving team experiences.

Here are some reflection questions for this chapter on healing yourself to enhance learning:

- Which of your beliefs and knowledge about health and well-being were confirmed in this chapter?
- What information about well-being surprised you and why?
- What new habits are you most interested in forming to change your SPICE score or improve your well-being and why?

CHAPTER 2

Self-Awareness for the Will to Endure Bad Teams

The team approach has become more commonplace in businesses, but it doesn't always work out for employees. The team that didn't work out for me formed after my division at a US-based Fortune 100 chemicals company was acquired by a multinational chemicals and pharmaceuticals giant. I agreed to stay on with the new company in order to receive an attractive retention bonus I was offered for completing at least one year working with the new company. The climate of the new company was so different from that of my old company that I felt like an unwelcome stranger in a new country. The change in climate was isolating and unnerving. Then, one day, the administrative assistant to the director of corporate research called me to schedule a meeting with the director. In the meeting, the director welcomed me to the company and asked if I would participate as a member of a new team to help accelerate product innovation at the company. The director said my work in this same area with my previous company would benefit the team. I accepted the invitation, hoping the new team would help me feel more connected to the new company and also (or mostly) because I was flattered to be recruited for my expertise. Sadly, the first team meeting I attended was by far the worst meeting I had ever attended.

The team leader did most of the talking and it sounded as though he was doing the bidding of a senior vice president (SVP) because when I offered an idea, I was told my idea did not fit with the SVP's plans. I regretted my decision to participate on that team at that first meeting and did not look forward to future team meetings. But the director of corporate research who got me on the team asked for my input in a separate private meeting. I could tell that the director valued my perspective not only on innovation but also on team leadership and team dynamics. So, even though I felt the team was a waste of my time, I continued to attend meetings so I could interact with the director to share my expertise in both innovation and team performance. In fact, my understanding of innovation and teamwork improved as a result of my regular conversations with the director about the frustrating team.

My will to participate in that bad team came from the opportunity to learn more about innovation and team performance through interaction with the director, a fellow frustrated team member. While the team did not perform to its potential, I was fulfilling my passion for learning. In addition, the director valued my innovation experience even though politics prevented that team from being a good way to incorporate my experience into the company's approach to product innovation. I endured those team meetings so I could learn and improve my understanding of innovation and teamwork by commiserating with an organizational leader. Several years later, that same organizational leader would recruit me to be a member of a new innovation organization being created and led by him.

Self-awareness is needed for the will to endure bad teams because it is the source of motivation needed to excel in teamwork even when bad teams happen to good people. Scientists understand more about motivation in the workplace now than was understood when I was recruited to my bad team experience more than twenty-five years ago. For example, workplace motivation can come from doing work that you find rewarding or from receiving an external reward like a big raise, a new promotion, or professional recognition. Doing work you find rewarding is an example of an intrinsic reward, like my participating in a bad team so I could learn from another team member because I love to learn. External rewards like raises or being recruited for a plum job years after my bad team experience are examples of extrinsic rewards. Different research studies have shown that extrinsic rewards increase the performance of straightforward tasks, whereas intrinsic rewards are needed to increase the performance of difficult tasks requiring original thinking.[1] In fact, extrinsic rewards have been shown to decrease the performance of challenging tasks that require critical thinking and creativity. Intrinsic rewards are needed for teamwork because working with others is hard work for your brain. Intrinsic rewards come from advancing your purpose, acting consistent with your values and personality, and using your strengths to benefit others. Self-awareness is needed to determine your purpose, values, personality, and strengths.

The importance of intrinsic rewards at work is predicted to grow as the economy transitions from the current predominantly information economy to the new proposed purpose economy over the next decade.[2] An example of an intrinsic reward that improves the performance of work requiring creativity and problem solving is having a sense of purpose toward that work. The move toward a new purpose economy has been hinted at by different authors[3] and celebrities.[4] A sense of purpose means you understand the role your work plays in improving the quality of life for others. Research shows that people with a sense of purpose have improved health and higher satisfaction with their life and work than those who

...rpose. In fact, a survey of thousands of
... the highest performers were those who
...efits to others with efficiency.[5] One way
...efits to others—and one step for a will to
...ng a sense of purpose in the workplace.

...RPOSE AND TEAMWORK

The "why" of your life is your sense of purpose. If you can articulate your purpose, then you can craft your participation in teams
toward the types of work tasks that bring you a sense of fulfillment
... growing body of research shows that a sense
... health, physical health, and quality
... that knowing your purpose will en-
... too. Ironically, doing the introspec-
... purpose helps increase interactions
... cus because benefitting others is at the

... simply an abstraction of what you are
... to find new ways to improve on what
you do well. My favorite example of purpose comes from *National
Geographic* photographer Dewitt Jones who made a video called
"Celebrate What's Right with the World." The title of the video is
Dewitt's six-word purpose statement. Dewitt discovered his purpose from a frustrating experience that he was able to turn around.
Specifically, he wanted to take a picture of a field of wildflowers,
but when he arrived at the field, the lighting wasn't quite right so he
decided to return later. When he went back to photograph the field
on a beautiful sunny day, he was frustrated to find that the field of
wildflowers was now a field of puff balls, so the picture he had in
mind was no longer possible. Dewitt decided to explore some different perspectives to see whether he could salvage the disappointment

with a different photograph. He ended up taking a stunning photograph by positioning the camera beneath a puff ball toward the blue sky with puffy white clouds. Dewitt realized that looking past what had gone wrong for his planned picture and being open to what might be right with what was before him created an entirely new picture. He learned his purpose of celebrating what's right with the world helped him unleash his creativity as a photographer and excel in his profession.

A purpose helps professionals excel in their profession because it puts you in touch with your source of passion and interest or with what you are wired to become. If you combine your source of passion and interest with what you do best, then you become unstoppable. Oprah Winfrey has a passion for inspiring people to be their best self and a talent for telling the stories of others, which turned her into the media mogul she is today. Daniel Pink has a passion for understanding the world better to be able to live more fully and a talent for writing, which has turned him into a best-selling author several times over.[7] A purpose captures why you do what you do. Having the why creates a whole host of hows, why elses, and how elses to fill your life with meaning in a myriad of different ways.

The process of finding your purpose starts with self-discovery because this personal discovery is required to understand your sources of motivation. The self-discovery techniques shared here help you categorize the types of work tasks and activities that bring personal satisfaction and meaning to you. I found that categorizing the types of work that bring me meaning served as helpful prework to a purpose exercise. There are several techniques and tools for self-discovery. I share four simple self-discovery tools here that I have used for understanding career aspirations, but other techniques and tools may resonate more with you and your situation.

A simple self-discovery exercise is, each day for at least a week, to take inventory of the work tasks you loved versus the work tasks you hated. Describe the tasks with as much detail as possible so you can understand what you wrote when you look at the inventory later for analysis. Look for common elements or underlying themes for the work tasks you loved as clues for what brings you meaning.

A second self-discovery exercise is to prioritize the following six passions: developing yourself, reaching your goals, sharing yourself, following your intuition, searching for meaning, and leaving a legacy.[8] It is helpful to know which one of these passions is most important to you when you are writing your purpose statement because they are the key types of work motivation. Each of these passions is worthy on its own merit, so prioritizing them helps you crystallize what brings you the most meaning without worrying about what others will think. I found it helpful to first select the most and least important passions in the list. For me, developing myself is most important, and following my intuition is least important. Then I was able to order the remaining four passions from highest to lowest priority between the passion I selected as most important and the passion I selected as least important. Second for me is sharing myself, third is reaching my goals, fourth is searching for meaning, and fifth is leaving a legacy. This prioritization helped me direct my high ambition toward the type of work that would also bring me personal fulfillment. Once you have prioritized them, you can explore how to pursue your top passions more in your work or in your teams to increase the satisfaction you can get from your work.

A third self-discovery exercise is to articulate your career motive from one of the following four categories:[9]

- Linear: success is moving up the corporate ladder to increase positional power to achieve important accomplishments and gain prestige.

- Expert: success is being recognized by peers as the expert and pursuing opportunities that further develop competence and expertise to have a secure and stable career.
- Spiral: success is being able to move from one position to a different but usually broader position that requires self-development, the development of new skills built on existing capabilities, the use of creativity, and often helping others grow and develop.
- Roamer: success is being able to change jobs frequently, typically every two years, and having high independence and variety in the search for self-identity and challenge.

My career motive is best described as roamer, and this realization helped release me from the peer pressure I felt to climb the corporate ladder in a linear fashion. Knowing your career motive helps guide career decisions and enables you to customize a path for career progression that will bring you meaning.

A fourth self-discovery exercise is to understand your desires.[10] Your desires are about why you should do what you want to do. The first step is to list every desire that you can think of without editing the list. The second step is to categorize each item on the list as either a true desire or a wish. A true desire is something you are willing to work on now to achieve, whereas a wish is something that you are not ready to work on yet. Next, categorize the desires into ten or fewer different types of desires to make the list more manageable. Finally, use the five whys technique to explore the abstract desires behind your list of wishes. For each wish, ask, "Why am I attracted to this" repeatedly until you can decide if that wish falls into an existing desire category or warrants a new desire category. Repeat the five whys technique for all the wishes on your list. Finally, look for clues in the abstract desires for what brings you the most meaning and find ways to pursue these sources of meaning in your work.

You are ready for a purpose exercise after you have spent enough time with self-discovery to better understand your sources of work motivation and meaning. There are also many different ways to articulate a purpose. In my most recent purpose exercise, I started by making a list of my most rewarding workplace experiences—those experiences that gave me a sense of accomplishment and contribution. I knew I had a good list when I got excited and energized recounting the experiences on the list. Next, I used questioning to distill the experiences on my list down to a more abstract concept. For each experience on the list, I asked, "Why was that rewarding?" or "Why was that impactful?" over and over again to distill it down to a few words. Next, I looked for common or similar words across all the experiences on my list. Finally, I used the common and similar words to articulate a purpose statement. My goal was to use the same format as Dewitt Jones's purpose statement: six words starting with an inspiring verb and using words meaningful to me and to the contribution I felt capable of making for the world. The purpose statement I came up with is as follows: *igniting the power of human connection*. This purpose statement may sound ridiculous to you, but it gets me up in the morning and gets me motivated when I encounter barriers in my work.

For comparison, I used a different process to write a purpose statement about seventeen years ago. This process was inspired by Peter Senge's view of personal mastery.[11] First, I wrote everything I could think of about what I wanted out of a career. Second, I wrote what I wanted for each of the following nine categories: self-image, tangibles, home, health, relationships, work, personal pursuits, community, and other. Third, I looked at what I wrote for each category and analyzed the content for relevance and benefits. For example, I asked myself: "If I could have what I wrote for that

categ   –yes or no?" If I said yes to any
aspec   ry, then I imagined I had what
I said   s that would bring me. Finally,
I revi   nd wrote my life purpose from
the c   nefits. The life purpose I wrote
at th   rpose is to show how fun and
rewa................. .. .. results in every facet of life (work
life, home life, spiritual life, and community life) through hard work,
respect for others, and collaboration. This earlier version of my purpose aligns with my more abstract and recent version to ignite the
power of human connection because purpose is what you are wired
to become from birth.

There is no right or wrong way to write a purpose statement, as
long as you put in the effort to learn enough about your sources of
motivation a   ʟ   ʟ   ʟ   ʟ   ire you to be your best
self. A good ɩ   o see the world from a
different pers   that increase your contribution and   es possibility. Without
change, ther   ay forward to a more
fulfilling life.   think change is bad,[12]
change is the   I resonate with Dewitt
Jones's appro   t to be the best for the
world rather   our talent in the world.
A sense of purpose can be a powerful tool for you to channel your
strengths and skills to be your best self and to make the best of bad
teams that happen to you. A sense of purpose also directs ways that
your identity can lead to meaningful work.

IDENTITY AND TEAMWORK

Another step for a will to endure bad teams other than articulating
your purpose is to explore your identity through the lens of your

core values and personality. Your purpose uncovers the meaning or "why" of your work while your values and personality reveal your unique identity and approach to your work. Your values and personality shape your behavior and thinking whether you are aware of them or not. Your values and personality are the types of information that you don't tend to verbalize and often are things you are not consciously aware of unless you've done the work to identify them.

In my first corporate job out of graduate school, I worked in a research center that served all the different businesses in the company. My boss's boss, a senior manager, would regularly check in on me to see how things were going. On one such occasion, I mentioned the challenges I was having interacting with one of the chemists in the group I had been assigned to work with on a project. The manager explained that different people value different things in the workplace and perhaps the difficulty was due to such differences. He then introduced me to a personality assessment called the Myers-Briggs Type Indicator to learn more about myself and what I value in the workplace. He said it might even help me interact better with people different from me in the workplace, like the chemist.

You can choose from many different personality profilers that assess your personal preferences and attributes for different situations. While an individual is too complex to be put in the box of any given personality profiler result, profiler findings can provide useful insights about you and about interacting with others. I have experience using three different personality profilers. They are the ones I am most familiar with, but they are not the only ones or the best ones available. That being said, you also need to be aware of a couple of caveats with regards to personality assessments.

The first caveat for personality profilers is that many of them lack scientific validity because they are self-report tools, and self-reporting can be influenced by a number of different factors.[13] So a personality profiler should be viewed as a tool for structured self-reflection and a gateway to studies based on the profiler that may or may not be helpful to you. If you find that a personality assessment is not helpful to self-understanding, then you might try a different one. I recommend you try personality triangulation by taking at least three different personality assessments you find helpful to increase understanding about your unique personality.

A second caveat for personality assessment is that you get only a slice of information about yourself and others because people are more complex than can be represented by a single personality profiler. Knowing your personality result and that of others for a given assessment can give you some clues as to how to optimize your interaction with another person, but it will not give you all the answers.

A third caveat for personality assessment is getting overconfident with your ability to assess other people's personalities with respect to a given profiler. People are very good at projecting an image of themselves that they want others to have of them while hiding their true selves. A person can be vulnerable to projecting an image different from who they truly are when they feel they don't belong and are trying to fit in. Not only can others fool you about their true personality, but people are not as good as they might think they are at interpreting the behaviors of others because of the tendency for all of us to overestimate our abilities.

A final caveat for personality assessment is your intended use and the intended use by others of this personality information.[14] Personality information can be used for selfish gains, or it can be used in productive, respectful, and appropriate ways. You need to be accepting of other people, especially those who are different from you so that you can use personality profiles in responsible and respectful ways. In fact, if you are accepting and genuinely curious about how other people are different from you, then you can improve your relationships with others and increase your performance in the workplace.

The first of my personality trifecta is the Myers-Briggs Type Indicator (or MBTI), mentioned previously, which has been the most popular personality profiler used by organizations and individuals since 1962.[15] As a result, many books and articles have been published about how to use knowledge about MBTI types to improve your effectiveness in the workplace and in interacting with others.

The first time I took MBTI, I used a simple, self-scoring version of the personality test and I typed as an ENFJ.[16] This means I tend to be extroverted (E), see the forest through the trees (N for sensing), base decisions on feelings (F), and use checklists (J for judging). The ENFJ type is referred to as the teacher.[17] This result was interesting to me because around fifty years ago I remember teaching my youngest brother what I learned in school each day before he started school.

I would come to think about MBTI a second time when I was selected for a corporate leadership development program at Notre Dame University. This time I took the full-blown version, which was graded by a consultant certified to administer the test. I still typed as an ENFJ, but the consultant greatly expounded on how MBTI could be put to use in the workplace. She provided us with tables of behavioral cues to be able to estimate the personality tendencies of our coworkers and bosses. She also provided tactics to communicate better and be more influential with people who are different from us within the context of MBTI types. I remember learning that the biggest gulf to cross in getting along with a coworker is the S-N dimension of MBTI for sensors (S) and intuitives (N). For example, in terms of persuasion, intuitives (N) like to see the big picture first while sensors (S) like to see a step-by-step explanation. I realized that this difference was causing my frustration trying to plan a meeting with a coworker whom I surmised had a sensor tendency compared to my intuitive tendency. In the next meeting with the coworker, I explained that I needed to understand the outcomes for the meeting before I could draft the step-by-step process needed to achieve those outcomes. We worked together great after getting over that hurdle!

Knowing your MBTI profile helps you perform at your best ability because the profile gives you clues on how to compensate for the failure of your natural tendencies to resolve challenging interactions. For example, if you are struggling with how to resolve a conflict with another person, then you can look up your conflict triggers[18] and tendencies in conflict situations[19] according to your MBTI profile. You can step through your conflict triggers to see whether you have a need that is not being fulfilled for clues on how to resolve the conflict. A conflict trigger for me as an ENFJ is exclusion, so I can explore if my need for inclusion is not being met. Alternatively, you can consider how to better use your natural strengths or compensate for your natural weaknesses according to your profile to resolve the conflict situation. I tend to internalize personal criticism, which may be appropriate when the relationship is more important than the conflict but is not appropriate when my perspective is important to the welfare of others. There are also resources according to the MBTI profile to help improve your approach to building relationships, making decisions, responding to change, and working in teams.[20]

The second of my personality trifecta is the Enneagram Personality Portraits Inventory and Profile.[21] This personality profiler has been described as similar to the MBTI but focused on how you can enhance your interactions with others. The version of the Enneagram that I took in 1998 had the following nine styles:
- 1s: Perfecters, Quality Performers, Stabilizers
- 2s: Carers, Helpers, Supporters
- 3s: Achievers, Producers, Motivators

- 4s: Creators, Expressionists, Individualists
- 5s: Observers, Thinkers, Systematizers
- 6s: Groupists, Relaters, Teamsters
- 7s: Cheerers, Animators, Cheerleaders
- 8s: Challengers, Asserters, Directors
- 9s: Acceptors, Receptionists, Reconcilers

For each of these nine Enneagram types, there is a description of personality, work style, leadership style, and directions for growth and decline relative to the other Enneagram types. I typed as a 4, and a 4's personality is described as naturally introspective. For work style, 4s tend to be expressive in communicating with others, imaginative in their approach to tasks, and motivated by work that offers the opportunity for recognition especially by important people. For leadership, 4s are sensitive to others' feelings and tend to sound out feelings before taking action or making decisions. My Enneagram type pointed to the need to be cautious about whom I expressed my feelings as a leader because not everyone in the workplace had my best interests in mind. Your Enneagram type is a way to prioritize your development needs and strengths in interacting with others.

The third of my personality trifecta is the Emotional Intelligence Map.[22] This personality profiler assesses the competencies and skills for individual emotional intelligence and for the ecosystem of emotional intelligence, which includes the outcomes, values, behaviors, and attitudes expected of those who practice high emotional intelligence and the current stress context for the test taker. From this personality profiler, I was surprised to discover that I was not comfortable making decisions about balance between work life and personal life. I also learned that I did not have enough awareness of my greatest sources of stress. As a result, I started to talk through decisions about balance between work life and personal life with trusted others. I also learned to be aware of my physical signs of stress, which for me is tenseness in my shoulders, and to take steps to address the stress when it appeared; for example, I go for a walk or watch a movie. Finally, I learned two areas needing personal development were handling conflict constructively and visualizing desired goals and results. For example, I needed to develop poise by not letting emotion show on my face and pay attention to my emotional reaction when someone disagreed with me. The Emotional Intelligence Map provides the top ways you can improve your emotional intelligence within your current situation.

The more you learn about your personality, the more you are able to behave consistently with it. Similarly, if you know your values, then you are more likely to behave consistently with those values. Consistency between your behavior and who you are is important to feeling comfortable, healthy, and satisfied with life.[23] In fact, inconsistency between behavior and your true identity creates internal psychological stress from a brain state called cognitive dissonance, which your brain must resolve.[24] Psychological stress caused by the behaviors of others in the workplace is the biggest source of stress for workers today.[25] Your brain does not like psychological stress, and your body will suffer if you cannot find ways to dissipate it. By knowing your personality and values, you can avoid internal stress and dissipate external psychological stress by keeping your behaviors consistent with your identity despite the behaviors of others.

When I found out that the position of eBusiness head was open, I was so excited because the person in the job had left the company. I had worked the longest in the eBusiness group, had the most success recruiting customers to use the eBusiness platform, and was the most highly regarded by the developers. The eBusiness platform developers valued me because I included them in the recruitment of customers, which gave them ideas for improved features. I felt that I was the obvious choice to succeed as eBusiness head based on my track record. Then I received the devastating news that the job had been filled by someone else! How was it possible that I had not been selected for the job? When my personal career coach asked me if I had made my desire for the job known to the decision maker for the position, I realized that I had not. While I felt entitled to earn the promotion, I had not made the effort to get it, a behavior that is inconsistent with my strong work ethic. I did not work toward winning that better job—someone else did. This inconsistency between my value for hard work and not working to get the job I wanted caused me a high degree of internal psychological stress. Fortunately, I learned from my mistake and boldly went after every job I wanted from that point forward in my career.

Taking the time to learn about and articulate your values will help you avoid and address sources of psychological stress in the workplace. In addition, values help us work with others effectively. For example, when we discover a value we have in common with another person, this is a powerful way to build trust and connect with that person. Similarly, we tend to attract others to us when we act consistent with our values. I have learned that no worthwhile accomplishment is possible without others, so knowing your values can move you closer to meaningful contribution through others.

Moreover, when we know our values, we are more resilient against people trying to influence us to do things that may not be in our best interest or in the best interest of the organization. When we are not aware of our true values, we can buy into the manipulative rationalization of another person. For example, I was not aware of my value to give love to others when a childhood friend convinced me to egg a neighbor's house one Halloween. Her rationalization was that one of the boys who lived in the house acted like a know-it-all and made her look stupid, which really irritated her. Not only did I throw an egg at the house, but the man of the house caught me and had tears in his eyes when he asked me why

I would do that to his home. I still feel bad about that behavior! Values, whether we are aware of them or not, play an important role in how we interact with others.

There is no one set of "correct" values because we are all wired differently and we all have different life experiences that shape our values. Of course, there are values that many of us share, but how we prioritize and behave according to our values is unique. The one thing that makes us the same is that we are different.

I learned a simple way to identify and prioritize values from an exercise I did as part of a group coaching experience.[26] We started with a set of personal value cards that we made from a PDF file.[27] There were eighty-three cards in the personal values deck plus three blank cards to fill in values that might be missing. The first step was to sort the cards into three piles. One pile was "not important to me," a second pile was "important to me," and the third pile was "very important to me." The second step was to reduce the number of cards in the "very important to me" pile down to no more than ten cards. The approach that helped me in this prioritization task was to ask: "Can I live a fulfilling life without this value?" The final step was to document values in a form that can be referenced as needed. I found it helpful to name the value and include a brief statement of why that value is important to me or what that value enables me to do that is important to me. For example, one of my values is knowledge because I want to learn and share knowledge and wisdom with others who might benefit. Value assessments, such as the Personal Values Assessment (PVA), also are available as an alternative method to identify your values.[28]

You can learn about your personality and values in many different ways. If you have a high degree of self-awareness, then you may need to do only one personality assessment and one value assessment to confirm what you already understand about your unique identity. For others who have lower self-awareness, several personality and value assessments may be needed to home in on their unique identity. One benefit of better understanding your identity is to minimize sources of internal and external psychological stress that come from behaving and thinking in ways at odds with your genuine values and personality. A second benefit of uncovering your values and personality is increasing your motivation to work in ways that align with your identity. A final benefit is deploying your strengths in ways you can be proud of in pursuing your purpose.

PERSONAL STRENGTHS AND TEAMWORK

A third step for a will to endure bad teams is to understand the strengths you can bring to teamwork. Regarding strengths, optimists, who see the glass as half full, would say that knowing your strengths enables you to use them more and find more success in everything you do. But pessimists, who see the glass as half empty, would say that knowing your strengths helps you identify your weaknesses so you can improve on or avoid them. There is some truth to both viewpoints. From the optimistic perspective, knowing your strengths enables you to find success by selecting team tasks, job assignments, and career opportunities that align with your strengths. And if you get to use a lot of strengths in your job, then you are more likely to find fulfillment and satisfaction in your job. On the other hand, from the pessimistic perspective, knowing your strengths can reveal your weaknesses and blind spots. I am not a strong proponent of improving on your vulnerabilities unless one or more of them is getting in the way of being able to do a satisfactory job. I am, however, a strong proponent of finding others who have strengths where you have vulnerabilities and then collaborating with them to compensate for those vulnerabilities and vice versa for the other person. You can find fulfillment and satisfaction in an organization by identifying your strengths, and you can improve your performance by being aware of your vulnerabilities.

Research shows that identifying your strengths can lead to a short-term improvement of mood and confidence. However, long-term psychological benefits are only possible from identifying and then actively using your strengths.[29] Therefore, you need an action plan for how you plan to use your identified strengths to get the most benefit out of an exercise to identify them.

I have used five techniques for different types of strength identification over the course of my career amid the myriad of tools and techniques available. I'm not saying these are the best tools and techniques, and they certainly aren't the only ones available for strength identification. They are just the tools and techniques that I am familiar with based on experience. Also, keep in mind that another way to learn about your strengths and weaknesses is through personality profilers, as described previously. You can see if any of these tools resonate with you or inspire you to find another method to identify the types of strengths you are most interested in exploring.

One tool I have used to identify strengths is an accomplishments inventory to keep a running record of significant career accomplishments that can be interpreted to find strengths. The inventory tracks accomplishments with a name, a description, and an explanation of significance. For example, the accomplishment of prototyping a draft website design in Excel was significant because the prototype was successful in enrolling the support of key stakeholders. A detailed description of this accomplishment is as follows: "Using Excel to prototype the draft design of a revised technical product website in order to gather input from industry, product, and technology managers for the new navigation planned for the website. The prototype was a great way to clarify exactly what the project team was looking for from the managers in a way that they could see why it was important." The more detailed the description, the better to overcome the tendency to take our strengths for granted. Underlying themes for this accomplishment are working through challenges with others and identifying new ideas to resolve challenges that represent strengths, such as collaboration and process innovation. This tool helps you focus on projects and aspects of work assignments where your strengths can enable you to contribute the most.

A second tool I have used is the networking profile self-assessment.[30] This self-assessment has fifty-five items based on fifty-five ways to become a more powerful networker. This tool is a way to identify your networking strengths. It is also a good resource on ways to get new ideas from others when you are stuck on a problem or work assignment.

A third tool I have used is called the MAPP assessment.[31] MAPP is an acronym for Motivated Appraisal of Personal Potential. I took the MAPP assessment back in 2004. The results predicted the types of tasks that I would most like to perform based on the motivations and preferences revealed by the assessment. These results also provided the following: how I prefer to perform tasks, my aptitude or degree of talent for performing different tasks, how I relate to people, how I relate to physical objects, my preferred ways of thinking, how I apply my thinking, how I relate to math and language, and top career areas I should consider. Fortunately, business consulting and writing were in my top ten career areas because that is what I am now doing! Three key strengths I learned about myself from MAPP were my abilities for influential communication of ideas to help do good in the world, fast learning, and generation of new and useful ideas. This tool helps you select career and project opportunities most in alignment with your working style and strengths.

A fourth tool that I have used is the thinking talents exercise first introduced to me by neuroscientist Dr. Dawna Markova and her business partner, Angie McArthur.[32] A thinking talent is a mental skill that energizes you when you are performing that skill. Markova and MacArthur provide guidance on how thinking talents can be used to improve interactions with others in their book *Collaborative Intelligence*. For example, you can improve your ability to influence others by diagnosing the other person's thinking talents and then adjusting your idea or proposal to appeal to the other person's thinking talents.

A fifth tool for identifying strengths is a do-it-yourself version of a method I experienced in an executive leadership program while at Bayer Corporation. The name of this technique is the Reflected Best Self exercise.[33] The first step is getting input from a diverse group of people who know you well both inside and outside of work. The input needs to identify your strengths with examples of how you used those strengths in a way that was meaningful to them or to their group or organization. The good news is that email works great for this first step to get the input in a digital format! The second step is to look for common themes across the input. For example, you can cut and paste the feedback received into a mind map application like Mind Manager[34] and then sort the feedback into common themes and capture insights. The third step is to write a description of your "best self" based on the feedback and your insights. The final step is to redesign your job description to incorporate what you have learned about what you are good at and what you need to be your best self.

Self-awareness directed at discovering your purpose, values, personality, and strengths helps you redirect a bad team experience to something that is valuable to you. However, if you take one more step to develop other-awareness, then the potential to transform a team experience exists. Scientists who study other-awareness call it Theory of Mind (ToM) skill.

THEORY OF MIND AND TEAMWORK

Work that articulates your purpose, explores your identity, and reveals your strengths maximizes your performance on a team when you can align your participation with these sources of motivation. Although this work on who you are provides the motivation to help endure a bad team, it is not always sufficient to survive one. Surviving a bad team takes accepting what you can and can't control about the team. A team is bad because the behavior of one or more other people is limiting its performance. You can control your response to another person's behavior consistent with your identity, but there may be more you can control in a bad team. However, you won't be able to understand what you can and can't control on a bad team without understanding the reason behind another person's behavior.

Scientists can measure the collective intelligence of a team to predict a team's performance on group tasks much like IQ predicts an individual's performance on learning tasks.[35] It is noteworthy that no correlation has been found between the IQ of team members and collective intelligence. But a correlation has been found between the Reading-the-Mind-in-the-Eyes score of members and collective intelligence, even for virtual groups. Reading-the-Mind-in-the-Eyes is one of the most common tests researchers have used to measure Theory of Mind skill.[36] ToM is the ability to understand another person's mental state so that you can interpret, explain, and predict their behavior. An increased understanding of how to measure and develop ToM skill is an active area of research to identify and treat various chronic mental conditions in adults, including autism spectrum disorder and schizophrenia.[37]

It is not too surprising that high-performance teamwork depends more on Theory of Mind skill than on intellect because it is the misinterpretation of another's intentions, not their intellect, that leads to bad teams. I remember leading a meeting to discuss a new proposed project to coordinate life cycle assessment (LCA) efforts across businesses and across countries at our organization. I invited the local LCA expert, whom I had gotten to know well from my business area, to the meeting for his perspective and input. The expert expressed anger at the meeting, saying that no committee was going to tell him how to do his job or get between him and the people who needed his expertise. I could have defended the intention of the project, but doing so would not have addressed the expert's mistrust. The expert needed a response based on his mental state of feeling his identity as an LCA expert was being questioned and threatened. Instead, I first thanked him for his input as an expert to show respect for his technical expertise. I next apologized for my miscommunication of the objectives for the planned project because I did not want him to feel wrong, which would further increase his feelings of anger. Finally, I explained how the planned project would support his expertise in the long run. For example, the project would increase awareness for the value that LCA brings so that the expert could get more resources to generate the data needed. The project went forward, and down the road I would learn about the benefits that this expert and other LCA experts at the organization received in learning from each other.

In my experience, ToM skill, or the ability to understand another person's mental state, is important to teamwork because being able to factor in a person's mental state to team communications is powerful. Mental states, and especially feelings, in response to proposed actions and decisions by a team and its members provide important information that can make the difference between success and failure. ToM skill is what enables a person to tease out the important and nonimportant information from a team member's reaction, especially when the reaction is disruptive to a meeting. There is still a lot that scientists don't understand about ToM skill, but there is growing consensus on some of the component skills needed. For example, ToM skill correlates with IQ, but IQ alone is not a sufficient condition for ToM skill. In addition, ToM skill takes the ability to inhibit your own perspective so that you can hold the perspectives of others in working memory for consideration. It also takes the ability to recognize and address discrepancies between internal expectations and external reality.[38] Finally, this skill can be developed by applying what is learned from simple examples in a training setting to the real world.[39]

There is a relationship between ToM skill and the three components of motivation: your purpose, identity, and strengths. For example, ToM skill is an important strength needed in team members for high-performance teamwork, and purpose and ToM skill go hand-in-hand. If you have a sense of purpose, then you need to develop ToM skill to live your purpose and realize the benefits of being purpose-driven. This skill also helps you address underlying differences in values, personality, and strengths with other people.

The irony is we need others to know who we truly are, and we need to know who we are to best interact with others. We think we know who we are, but the only way to truly know who we are is to have others hold up a mirror to our behaviors and attitudes. Who we are may not be who we think we are. Who we are is how we show up to others.

There are both proactive motives, like wanting to be the best for the world, and reactive motives, like feeling stuck or frustrated in your career, for personal career development. I have learned that proactive motives have been more powerful than reactive motives for my career development. In addition, the executives who have most inspired me by their accomplishments also espouse proactive motives. So when you are feeling reactive motives in your work or on a team, you might try looking for proactive motives to reach for the stars. These motives come from your personal purpose, values, preferences, and strengths. Proactive motives come from knowing and being your true self. They also fuel a desire to develop ToM skill so you can better predict and understand the behaviors of others. Being able to predict and understand the behavior of others is a powerful tool for team leadership discussed in the next chapter.

Here are some reflection questions for this chapter on self-awareness to enhance learning:

- What have been your most and least valuable experiences with self-assessments and why?
- What information about self-awareness intrigued you and why?
- What actions do you think you can take to enhance your motivation to work in teams and why?

CHAPTER 3

Troubleshooting
Team Leadership

Team leaders transport team members to a new intellectual, emotional, conceptual, or physical place. Effective leaders can change people's way of thinking and acting. It is hard enough to change yourself, let alone change others. I don't like to change unless I have to, but I like it less when someone else tries to make me change. Team leadership is challenging because leaders are tasked with convincing others to change their minds, perspectives, and behaviors.

Team leaders are like snowflakes: every snowflake is unique, and each leader is unique. The good news about leadership is there is no one right approach. The bad news is there is no one right approach. Leadership would be so much easier if there was just one way to do it.

An efficient approach to team leadership is for team leaders to use their personal leadership style and adjust their style as needed to address problems. Leaders need to identify and correct problems with their personal leadership style to remain effective over time. They must lead in a way that is consistent with who they are as individuals because authenticity is a key ingredient to building trust with others. The human brain can detect a phony from a mile away, and I don't know about you, but I don't trust a phony. Team members are going to be very careful about engaging with a leader they don't trust. These leaders must engage members for team performance to be high, but engagement is not the only problem that they face.

SYMPTOMS OF TEAM LEADERSHIP PROBLEMS

Sometimes a team leader is aware of their leadership problems and sometimes not—it's no fun being the cause of a problem and not knowing it! The good news is that signs team leadership is going wrong enable a leader to rescue a team from imminent or longer-term demise. The signs that leadership is going wrong can be boiled down to three symptoms.

The first symptom is the team leader experiences negative emotion during a team meeting. For example, a leader can experience anger with confrontation by a team member, annoyance with member behavior, disgust with problems that arise, and despair with how a meeting is going. For example, one way to frustrate a leader is, after several meetings, a member disagreeing with one or more of the team's goals. Getting goals correct is one of the most important steps to team performance, so goal conflict within the team can be a real setback. But a leader who sees goals as a reflection of their performance as a leader can interpret criticism of goals as a personal attack. Luckily, goals are different from setting a clear direction, and the latter is a distinct leadership responsibility. Setting a clear direction is a vision of what a better future looks like, whereas goals are the steps to get to that better future. So the team leader is accountable to the vision while the entire team is accountable to the team goals.

Another way that a team leader can experience negative emotion is by taking responsibility for the performance of team members. A leader taking responsibility for the performance of members is like a parent taking responsibility for the successes and failures of their child. A parent can create an environment for a child that is more conducive to success than to failure. Research shows that parents who are both demanding and supportive increase the skills children need to find success in life.[1] But children are responsible for the self-discipline needed for success and for the decisions they make and actions they take that shape their adult life. Similarly, leaders can create an environment for team performance to thrive, but they cannot control the performance of individual team members.

A team leader experiencing negative emotion is dissatisfied with team performance. But a leader's negative emotion is more damaging to performance than how team members are performing. Scientists have discovered that experiencing too little or too much emotion degrades cognitive performance.[2] The relationship between emotion and cognitive performance is called the performance-arousal curve. Further, the experience of negative emotion is faster, stronger, and longer lasting than the experience of positive emotion.[3] These research findings for negative emotion mean that experiencing high levels of negative emotion quickly degrades logical thinking. A leader must preserve logical thinking to interact with members in ways that increase team performance.

The second symptom that team leadership is going wrong is a team member experiencing negative emotion, which is a problem because that member's logical thinking is degraded according to the performance-arousal curve. This curve is an inverted-U relationship between cognitive performance on the vertical axis and level of emotion on the horizontal axis. Further, negative emotion expressed by a member can be compounded by a phenomenon known as emotional contagion. Emotional intelligence guru Daniel Goleman describes emotional contagion as the extent to which we experience other people's emotions.[4] Scientists have found that the stronger the emotion, the more contagious the emotion. Emotion is contagious: our brain is programmed to pay attention to emotion because emotion can indicate a threat to our survival. We notice another person experiencing strong emotion, especially negative emotion, because we need to understand what is going on and how we are affected. In fact, a caveat for team leaders is the tendency to catch negative emotions from team members.

The final symptom that team leadership is going wrong is apathy by one or more team members. For example, a team leader asks for input on a problem from members, and no one looks up from their cell phone. A lack of interest from members can mean they don't understand what the leader is asking for, don't see what is in it for them to share thoughts and ideas, or don't feel safe putting forth their thoughts and ideas. Members become hesitant to contribute for different reasons, but at the heart of this hesitancy is a process problem. This type of problem means the way the team leader is conducting the meeting is not producing the desired results.

A lack of interest by team members can be more sinister than a hesitancy to contribute due to a problem with how the meeting is being conducted. For example, members may withdraw from participating in a meeting if they are upset with or frustrated by the team leader and want the leader to fail. One way a leader can anger and frustrate members is by being demanding but unsupportive when support is needed. A leader who has produced results of value to the organization can become dependent on the good feelings that results can bring. Leaders who become dependent on results may distance themselves from failure by being demanding but unsupportive of members' performance. They can also get addicted to the good feelings of leadership success and stop taking the risks needed for the next big success because failure is no longer an option for them. A leader who avoids failure also avoids learning, creativity, and opportunities for future successes and increased impact.[5] Leaders who distance themselves from failure are limiting the results possible from the team—another source of frustration and anger for members.

The symptoms of a team leadership problem are negative emotions experienced by the team leader or a team member and withdrawal by one or more members. These problems are caused by the internal, external, and inherent challenges of leadership. The next section provides examples of these different types of leadership problems.

TYPES OF TEAM LEADERSHIP CHALLENGES

I had just finished graduate school and was full of ambition when I accepted a corporate position with Monsanto. After a couple of years, I was selected by Monsanto executive leadership to attend a leadership program at the Center for Creative Leadership (CCL).

The leadership program was an elaborate one-day role play. Program participants came from different companies all over the world. The CCL facilitator provided background for a fictional organization and a challenge that the organization was facing as the setting for the role play. Next, a CCL facilitator read different role descriptions for the role play, one at a time, and asked for a volunteer after each one. Typically, the first person to raise their hand would be assigned the role. I wanted a role that would challenge me so I could make the most out of the learning experience. When one of the CCL facilitators read the role of CEO, the room fell silent. A little voice inside my head told me to volunteer even though I knew I was not qualified. But the room stayed silent. My better judgment told me that the room was silent for a reason and I should not volunteer. But my ambition prevailed and I found myself raising my hand and being assigned the role. Participants were assigned offices, phones, and schedules according to their assigned roles.

From my schedule as mock CEO, I learned that I needed to prepare and deliver a motivating speech to the rest of the program participants as part of the role play. I remember being anxious about the speech I was expected to prepare and deliver. I also remember feeling like an imposter in the CEO's shoes; it was almost an out-of-body experience. I don't remember much about the role play except relief when it was over and an overall feeling that it had gone fairly well. Then the CCL facilitators delivered the news that our role play scored the lowest they had seen in the history of running this exercise. That is when the real learning began.

The CCL facilitators explained that the role play I had participated in as CEO had some hidden opportunities to deliver value that could be uncovered only by people from different functions talking to each other. Points were awarded for each hidden opportunity identified and harvested by role-play participants. But schedules were designed to keep participants focused inside their function. The CCL facilitators expected high performers to go beyond their responsibilities to deliver value because value correlates with the number of other people that benefit from your work. The more other people you can benefit in the workplace, the more value you can deliver to the organization.

The role play under my leadership failed in uncovering many of the hidden opportunities to deliver value. Although I didn't know it at the time, I had just experienced several internal leadership challenges. These types of challenges occur when lack of skill, experience, and knowledge act as barriers to leadership in a given situation. In the case of the CCL role play, my lack of skill in delivering speeches was a distraction from addressing the organization's problems. Further, my lack of experience finding opportunities to create value led to underperformance as a leader setting an example of and climate for collaboration. In addition to internal leadership challenges, there are external leadership challenges.

At Monsanto, the new director of research wanted to promote me from a senior researcher to a research manager as part of a reorganization. I was surprised and delighted because I had been a part of the organization for only three years at the time. I was given the largest and most diverse group to manage in the research organization. My research group included PhD scientists doing polymer research, technical professionals providing support to technical marketing, technicians providing polymer processing support, and facility management.

One day after my promotion, my facility manager, a star performer in the department by every measure, came into my office agitated. He said that one of the group's contract technicians refused to wear safety shoes while operating polymer processing equipment—a violation of our safety policy. We hired our contract technicians from a local employer who supplied technical workers for temporary positions. I thanked my facility manager for bringing this issue to my attention and told him that I would address the situation.

I collaborated with the contract technician's employer to develop a plan to address the reported safety shoe violations. The explanation the contract technician provided for not wearing her safety shoes was that she had a foot condition that made the safety shoes uncomfortable to wear. I accompanied the contract technician to our safety shoe provider to make sure she was provided with adequate safety shoes for her foot condition. However, she was caught violating the safety shoe policy again two days later, so I terminated her employment as I had warned that I would do if she violated the policy again.

A couple of days afterward, I got a phone call from our company lawyer. The lawyer told me that the fired technician had filed a wrongful termination lawsuit against our company, claiming religious discrimination. I burst out laughing. Religious discrimination has nothing to do with not wearing safety shoes while operating polymer processing equipment! Thankfully, I had documented in great detail all my interactions with the contract technician and with her employer. I made copies of my documentation for our company's lawyer. Our lawyer used my documentation as proof of a valid termination of employment. As a result, the lawsuit filed by the disgruntled former contract technician was shown to have no basis and was dismissed from court proceedings.

External leadership challenges occur when the behavior of others or the situation creates barriers to leadership. Situations that can provide barriers to leadership include cost-cutting measures that impact a team, unrealistic schedules from top management, and project scope creep by customers. The shenanigans of the contract technician ended up being a significant drain on my time as a research manager even though my actions were appropriate to the situation. Sometimes leadership, like life, isn't fair. Thankfully, in the case of the irresponsible contract technician, the truth prevailed in the end.

Another challenge from my promotion to research manager was attending my first staff meeting. The director of research had the foresight to call me into his office before the meeting. The director explained that he was going to offer some advice to help me prepare for the meeting. He also said that if I found the advice helpful he would be willing to continue providing advice as long as I kept our mentoring meetings a secret. The director did not want the other technology managers to think that I was getting special treatment because of our mentoring relationship. In fact, the director was trying to level the playing field by removing barriers to my performance as the first and only female research manager. The advice he gave me in that first mentoring session still sticks: "You are walking into a room full of sharks. They will test you, and at the first sign of blood, they will attack. Don't let them see any blood."

And he was right. My male peers were brutal toward me in that first staff meeting. I had to excuse myself more than once to go cry in the bathroom and then recompose myself before returning to the meeting.

Leadership is not for the faint of heart. In addition to internal and external leadership challenges are inherent leadership challenges. These challenges occur when the resilience and discipline needed to bear the difficulties, burdens, and loneliness of being a leader are lacking. Inherent leadership challenges include unhealthy competition from peers, like my room full of sharks. Other inherent challenges are motivating yourself and others, avoiding complacency in the face of success, and avoiding hopelessness in the face of failure.

The good news is that a leader can employ various tactics to handle the internal, external, and intrinsic challenges of leadership. The tactics that have worked for me as a team leader are presented here by type of leadership challenge. They are based on how I learned to handle the top challenges I encountered leading teams. You are welcome to use these tactics as is and encouraged to customize and improve on them to suit your preferences and situation.

ADDRESSING INTERNAL LEADERSHIP CHALLENGES IN TEAMS

The research literature on leadership finds that the most effective leaders are excellent managers and excellent leaders. Leadership guru Peter Drucker said leadership is about determining the right results and management is about achieving results. Effective team leaders can identify the right results and can achieve them. Management and leadership both take people skills and a drive for results that deliver value from a systems point of view. If you don't treat people well in driving for results, then it is only a matter of time before those people will turn against you. For example, if you focus on results above all else, then the people commitment needed to support the results will wane over time as people get frustrated with not being recognized for their contribution. Further, if you don't pay attention to delivering value from a systems point of view in determining the right results, then the infrastructure needed to realize the right results will not be there. For example, investing significant resources to develop an innovative new product makes sense if there is a realistic potential for making a profit from selling the new product. Team leaders who see how people and results are related will benefit in the long term.

Both driving for results and exhibiting good people skills don't come naturally to leaders. Only 13 percent of 51,000 leaders were found to display strong abilities in both driving for results and having good people skills.[6] I have found two key approaches for team leaders to develop this rare combination of skills. The first approach is involving others to develop high-quality team goals that produce results. The second approach is using leadership mindsets that support the people skills needed to produce results.

A team leader is appointed because there is a vision of what a better future looks like that can't be realized by one person alone. Often it is not clear how to realize this vision because that is something that the team needs to figure out. Regardless, the leader needs to set and communicate a clear direction for the team. Setting a clear direction takes understanding what the current situation is and what the desired future state looks like. The leader can distill the team's direction into a list of proposed team goals. But input from team members is important to create high-quality team goals because different perspectives increase the value that can be produced by the team. In fact, the value that can be produced by the team can be increased even more by seeking and incorporating input from the team's key stakeholders. A large study of working professionals revealed that value is equal to benefits to others times quality times efficiency.[7] For a team, benefits to others are the benefits to the team's stakeholders or a representative sample of the people impacted by the team's outputs.

One tactic I have used to incorporate team member input into a team goal is a group exercise to test and address the quality of the goal. This tactic is based on a proven process from strategic planning.[8] It involves the following five steps, which are explained with examples in the ensuing paragraphs.

GROUP PROCESS TO IMPROVE TEAM GOALS

Step 1. Broad Goal Areas: Infinite Verb + Aim + Impact

Step 2. Objectives That Are SMART and Measure a Result or Impact

Step 3. Critical Success Factors for Pursuing Goals and Objectives

Step 4. Barriers to Pursuing Goals and Objectives

Step 5. Strategies: Finite Verb + Object + Purpose

The first of five steps to develop team goals is to write broad goals using the format of an infinite verb followed by a broad long-term aim that makes clear the impact of the goal on the group or organization. An infinite verb is one that has direction but no destination like *provide, promote, maximize, maintain,* or *foster.* A sample broad goal is "maximize awareness of our brand to drive business results." The infinite verb is *maximize,* the aim is *brand awareness,* and the impact is *business results.*

The second step is to identify objectives for the broad goals that satisfy the following three criteria: they measure a result or impact and not just an activity; they are SMART, an acronym for specific, measurable, achievable, relevant, and time-bound; and together, if achieved, they will accomplish the broad goal. A sample objective for the broad goal "maximize awareness of our brand to drive business results" is "use branded landing pages to track the effectiveness of five different approaches over the next twelve months to increase the enrollment of our online courses." This objective measures the effectiveness of different landing pages on enrollment in online courses. It is time-bound and specific enough to be measurable. This objective is also relevant to driving business results because online course enrollment is a source of business revenue.

The third step is to brainstorm critical success factors for the broad goals and objectives. Critical success factors are conditions that must be met to accomplish the objectives for the broad goal. Consider again the objective to "use branded landing pages to track the effectiveness of five different approaches over the next twelve months to increase the enrollment of our online courses." A sample critical success factor for this objective is to "find a landing page application that can track click-throughs to online course enrollment pages and revenues from completed online course enrollments."

The fourth step is to brainstorm barriers for the broad goals and objectives. Barriers answer the questions: "Why aren't we there yet? What is standing in our way?" Again, consider the objective to "use branded landing pages to track the effectiveness of five different approaches over the next twelve months to increase the enrollment of our online courses." A sample barrier for this objective is "no budget for a firm to design five different branded landing pages."

The final step is to brainstorm strategies for achieving the broad goals. Strategies are broad activities required to achieve an objective, create a critical condition, or overcome a barrier. The format for a strategy is a finite verb plus an object and a purpose. A finite verb is one that has a destination like *establish, develop, implement, build, create, educate, review, prepare,* or *define.* Consider how to overcome the barrier of "no budget for a firm to design five different branded landing pages." A sample strategy to overcome this barrier is to "secure a project budget for designing five different branded landing pages to drive online course enrollment." Strategies provide high-quality goals for teams.

Another tactic to incorporate team member input into a team goal is writing the goal to appeal to both sources of motivation for goal pursuit.[9] One source of motivation is moving toward something of value or that is beneficial. A second source of motivation is moving away from something that destroys value or is detrimental. Goals written to appeal to both sources of motivation for goal pursuit are better than those written to appeal to just one source. For example, a goal to create a proprietary application for idea generation is appealing to those who want to create a competitive advantage in innovation. However, a goal to establish a competitive idea generation system with benefits that outweigh costs still creates a competitive advantage in innovation but also avoids unnecessary costs.

A tactic to incorporate stakeholder input into team goals is to survey the stakeholders. Team stakeholders are the individuals who stand to benefit the most and lose the most from the team's work. For example, the stakeholders for a team charged with designing a new order placement application are existing customers and new potential customers. The team can take a "divide and conquer" approach like the following to interviewing stakeholders:

1. The team identifies their stakeholders—the individuals who stand to benefit the most and lose the most from the team's work. The team selects a representative sample of people for each type of stakeholder to provide input.

2. The team designs a set of open-ended questions to interview the representative sample of stakeholders and understand the specific ways in which the team's work can benefit them and cause concern for them.

3. The team divides the stakeholders among team members to conduct the interviews. The interviews are conducted and the input documented to bring back to the team.
4. The team reviews the input from the interviews and connects the input to the team's goals and objectives. New goals and objectives may be created for input that does not connect to existing team goals and objectives.
5. The team's goals and objectives are revised based on stakeholder input and consensus by the team.

Six team leader mindsets, described next, demonstrate the people skills required to lead teamwork that produces results. A mindset is a belief that is established and regularly practiced through repeated use. I have found that the absence of one or more of these six team leader mindsets causes leadership problems.

SIX TEAM LEADER MINDSETS

1. Share the Floor in Order for Team Impact to Soar
2. Start with Purpose and Trust, or Else Teamwork Is a Bust
3. When Wrong, Don't Stay There Long; Switch to Learn and Respect You Will Earn
4. A Plan Is Not Gold: Know When to Stick to It and When to Fold
5. Praise the Working Parts, Not the Smarts
6. Use Difference Causing Dislike to Fuel Curiosity for Skills to Like

---

The first team leader mindset for a high-performing team is to share the floor for team impact to soar. Research has shown that team performance correlates with the degree of equal participation across team members.[10] It is a myth and is detrimental to team performance for the team leader to have all the answers. In fact, research also shows that situational humility is a key aspect of high-performance teamwork.[11] Situational humility means that a team leader acknowledges that they don't have all the answers.

The second team leader mindset for a high-performing team is start with purpose and trust, or else teamwork is a bust. Neuroscience shows that joy and performance at work are the result of doing purpose-driven work with a trusted team.[12] Teamwork driven by a purpose provides a "why" for "what" needs to be done. Once all team members are convinced of the "why," an atmosphere of trust among members enables focus on "how" to achieve "what" must be implemented. Teamwork is an investment of time and intellect by members. You would not invest your hard-earned money without understanding why something is a good investment and how you will make money. Similarly, a leader should not expect a member to invest their time and intellect without that member understanding "why" doing so is a good investment and "how" a return on that investment will be achieved.

The third team leader mindset for a high-performing team is when wrong, don't stay there long; switch to learn and respect you will earn. A leader may be tempted to demonstrate their expertise and knowledge to team members. Demonstrating expertise and knowledge is one way to increase social status, which can trigger a reward response in the brain. A reward response causes the "feel good" neurotransmitter dopamine to be released in the brain, which leads to positive feelings like pleasure and satisfaction. Effective leaders focus on improving a meeting rather than on demonstrating their expertise and knowledge. The caveat is that a leader risks being wrong or putting forth a poor idea when focusing on improving a meeting. A leader's social status can decrease when they are wrong or share a bad idea, which can lead to a threat response in their brain. A threat response causes the neurotransmitter somatostatin to be released in the brain, which regulates the behavior needed to respond to the threat.[13] Next, the brain diverts oxygen and glucose away from the parts of the brain that support high-level thinking and to the parts of the brain and body needed to support the behavioral response.[14] We can say things we later regret when we feel threatened because less oxygen and glucose are flowing to power up the thinking part of the brain.

There is another choice, other than to feel threatened, when a team leader realizes they have said something wrong or have shared a bad idea. Leaders can view being wrong or sharing a bad idea as an opportunity to learn and improve their social status in the long term rather than as a threat in the short term. This mindset helps the leader avoid the allure of being right, which can make that person annoying to team members, especially if the leader seeks to prove others wrong. Further, the need to demonstrate knowledge and expertise can make a leader look insecure and degrade their effectiveness.

The fourth team leader mindset for a high-performing team is a plan is not gold: know when to stick to it and when to fold. This leadership mindset was expressed by US President Dwight D. Eisenhower as "plans are nothing; planning is everything."

I learned the fourth team leader mindset when, after an intensive three-day training session on facilitating creative problem solving, I was asked to facilitate a one-day workshop for the CEO and his staff. I applied what I had learned in my training to the planning and designing of the workshop. The morning of the workshop went very well under my leadership. But, in the afternoon, the CEO asked about drilling down on one of the ideas from the morning session, and I froze because this was a deviation from my plan. The CEO took over the meeting at that point. You can imagine how much of a failure I felt like at that point in the meeting. Fortunately,

I learned from this bad experience and have since developed the skills needed to be flexible in adjusting a facilitation plan on-the-fly as needed by participants.

A team leader who must deviate from their meeting plan when the team needs to go in a different direction can feel wrong, which can produce a threat response and lead to negative feelings. But a leader willing to change plans if a better path forward is revealed has the opportunity to learn something new about meeting process and improve as a leader. Planning for a team meeting is still important, but flexibility is even more important as a team becomes skilled at collaborating in a way that reveals new and potentially better solutions and approaches to their work. This mindset of "plan is not gold: know when to stick to it and when to fold" helps a team leader avoid the allure of controlling what others are doing. A leader who insists on controlling what the team is doing can look foolish when an opportunity for higher team performance is missed.

The fifth team leader mindset for a high-performing team is praise the working parts, not the smarts. Psychology research has shown that a person's mindset can help explain why people succeed or fail in school, in sports, in relationships, and in work.[15] Research studies have found that praising a person for their effort, hard work, and perseverance leads to higher performance because this type of praise promotes a growth mindset. A growth mindset is the belief that hard work can lead to improvement. But praising a person for a trait like intelligence or creativity leads to lower performance because this type of praise promotes a fixed mindset. A fixed mindset is the belief that a trait like intelligence or creativity is fixed, so there is a limit to how much you can improve. Praising team members for their hard work and efforts helps team leaders promote a growth mindset in members, and a growth mindset improves performance.

The final team leader mindset for a high-performing team is use difference causing dislike to fuel curiosity for skills to like.

This leadership mindset was expressed by US President Abraham Lincoln as "I don't like that man. I must get to know him better." It is said that curiosity killed the cat, which is why cats supposedly have nine lives! Curiosity may have nothing to do with cats; however, curiosity does have to do with threats and rewards. Neuroscience has revealed two types of curiosity depending on anticipation of a reward or response to a threat.[16] Reward-based curiosity produces a pleasant state because it is the type of curiosity that leads to learning something new and growing as a person. In fact, reward-based curiosity is one of two key ingredients that creates the psychological safety needed to take some risks and collaborate with strangers.[17] Reward-based curiosity lets a team leader listen with intent to understand a team member they may dislike or not know very well. This mindset helps team leaders avoid threat-based curiosity, which is curiosity in response to realizing a shortcoming relative to another person. Reward-based curiosity is being open to the benefits that others can bring, whereas threat-based curiosity is giving in to competing with others, which dissipates a team leader's cognitive abilities.

Many team leadership problems can be traced back to not practicing one of these six team leader mindsets. Leaders can be proactive and develop approaches to practice these mindsets in team meetings. They can also use these mindsets as a checklist after a meeting has occurred to troubleshoot problems that occurred in the meeting. Finally, a team member's motivation or performance may be impacted by the absence of one or more of these six team leader mindsets without the leader's awareness. Thus, leaders need to be open to one-on-one feedback from members outside meetings and to thoughtful tactics used by members in meetings to address leadership problems.

If a team member is demotivated because the team leader is not practicing one of the six team leader mindsets for high team performance, then the member can address the problem outside the meeting. That member can set up a private meeting with the leader to discuss team performance. The following is a proven method for a member to address a problem with a leader in a private meeting.

STEPS FOR TEAM MEMBER TO PROVIDE ONE-ON-ONE FEEDBACK TO TEAM LEADER

1. A team member needs to first ask permission from the team leader to share an observation to improve the member's performance on the team.
2. If permission is granted, then the team member describes the problematic behavior by the team leader and how that behavior impacts the member's performance.
3. The team member may wish to cite evidence supporting how a different behavior by the team leader can improve team performance.
4. The team member summarizes their feedback in the form of a problem statement to enable the team leader to have input on how to address the problem. A problem statement starts with a phrase like, "How to," "In what ways might," or "How might." An example is, "How might I not worry that my input will be put down by you during a meeting?"
5. The final step is for the team member to ask the team leader for ideas on how to address the problem. The member should also be ready to provide ideas in case the leader invites them to do so.

A team member can address a team leadership problem during a meeting if they have a thoughtful tactic to address the problem. A thoughtful tactic means the tactic addresses the various scenarios that can play out. For example, if the team leader is doing too much of the talking during a team meeting, then a member can raise their hand and ask for clarity on what type of input is needed from members. If the input needed is clarified, then the member can suggest a group process like going around the room to provide the input one member at a time. If no input is needed from members, then the member can suggest moving on to a topic that does require member input. If there are no other topics, then the member can propose ending the meeting until work requiring input from members becomes a priority. The member can explain to the team leader that there is no need to tie up the valuable time of the leader in a meeting with people who don't have the needed input.

This section provided tactics for team leaders and team members to address internal leadership challenges related to a lack of experience and skill by the leader. The next section provides tactics for a team leader to address the external leadership challenges of lackluster performance and disruptive behavior by team members.

ADDRESSING TEAM MEMBER NEEDS

Social situations like teamwork spark emotions, and while some emotions are helpful to performance, other emotions degrade performance. In fact, neuroscience reveals that social needs are the brain's top priority for our survival.[18] A team leader is in a unique position to impact the social needs of team members. Leaders who recognize and meet the social needs of members will be rewarded with satisfied and engaged members. However, leaders who violate the social needs of members, whether intentional or not, will trigger threat responses in members' brains, which can degrade high-level thinking ability. A member whose thinking ability has been compromised because of a threat state will have reduced ability to perform in meetings.

Three universal social needs are important to teams.[19] According to research, teams can't perform at a high level unless the social needs of all team members are being met. The three universal social needs for teams are the need for inclusion and respect, the need for control, and the need for a shared and accurate understanding of what is going on. Team leaders can use two approaches to address these universal social needs in teams. A direct approach is for the leader to identify threats to members' social needs and then remove or dissipate these threats. A proactive approach is for the leader to use team process to meet the social needs of members. We look at the direct approach of identifying and then removing or dissipating threats to members' social needs first.

A team leader needs to recognize when a team member's social needs have been threatened to be able to remove or dissipate a social needs threat. We experience negative emotion and either act out or withdraw from the social situation when one of our social needs has been threatened. For example, the need for respect can cause evaluation apprehension or the tendency to withdraw because you are worried about what the other people on the team will think about your input. The leader can watch for signs of negative emotion like anger, anxiety, fear, frustration, disappointment, discouragement, and sadness from members. Negative emotion can come across in the tone of voice, choice of words, facial expression, and behavior. The better a leader can identify their own emotions, the better that leader can understand and predict the emotions of others, like team members.[20] A leader can get better at identifying their emotions through practice. For example, they can carry a notebook to record what they are feeling and to explore what interactions triggered that feeling.

Once the team leader recognizes the signs of negative emotion in a team member that indicates a social needs threat, the leader can call for a break and approach the effected member one-on-one. The leader can say to the effected member: "You appear to have been offended in some way. Was something said at the meeting that was upsetting to you?" If the member answers no, then the leader can ask: "Was something said before the meeting that was upsetting to you?" If the member still answers no, then the leader can ask the member to describe how they are feeling and why they are feeling that way. If the member can describe how they are feeling, then sometimes this discussion is enough to dissipate the negative emotion.[21] But if the member answers yes to one of the first two questions, then the leader must ask more questions to determine which of the three social needs has been threatened. For example:

- To explore threats to the social need for inclusion and respect: "Did something happen to make you feel disrespected or not included?"
- To explore threats to the social need for control: "Did something happen that limited your contribution or created uncertainty for you?"
- To explore threats to the social need for shared understanding: "Did something happen that you did not understand or that was confusing?"

The team leader needs to ask for specifics about the source of the threat to be able to remove or dissipate the threat state of a team member. Further, the leader needs to be prepared to take responsibility if they are the one who violated one or more of the social needs of the member. The leader can offer an alternative interpretation for the member that removes the threat response once the source of the social needs threat is understood. Alternatively, they can provide a genuine statement that boosts one or more of the three social needs for that member to dissipate the threat response.

A threat state indicative of a social need not being met can be triggered by an unmet expectation. If an expectation is strong and rewarding, then when the expectation is not met, a threat state can ensue. I remember watching a football game between the New England Patriots and the Pittsburgh Steelers—in full disclosure, I am a Pittsburgh Steelers fan. At half-time, the Steelers were leading, so I decided that the Steelers were going to win. I was excited by the prospect of the Steelers winning because they had lost to the Patriots all four times the two teams had met over the previous four years. Thanks to a questionable ruling on the field (yes, I am still trying to justify my expectation), the Patriots eked out a win. I had never been in a fouler mood after a Steelers game than after that one. If the threat state of a team member is due to an unmet expectation, then the team leader needs to identify the expectation that was unmet and express genuine empathy for the resulting disappointment. Next, the leader can provide a genuine statement that boosts one or more of the social needs (inclusion and respect, control, shared understanding) for that member to dissipate the threat response.

Team leaders themselves are not immune to social needs threats. In this case, the leader needs to be able to recognize when they are experiencing a negative emotion and then call for a break. A social needs threat produces negative emotion, which can degrade high-level thinking ability—something a leader needs! During the break, the leader needs to assess and reappraise the situation to remove or dissipate the threat.

Process tactics also can be tried to mitigate the bad behavior that can result from social needs threats to one or more team members. These process tactics may have limited success unless the underlying cause of the social needs threat is identified and addressed. The tactics may also have limited success unless the negative emotion from the social needs threat has been dissipated for the effected member. The negative emotion needs to be dissipated enough for the effected member to not spread the negative emotion to other members and to not have their own cognitive capacity impaired.

One example of a way that a team member experiencing a social needs threat can act out is to have side conversations during the team meeting. A process tactic the team leader can use to address side conversations starts with pointing out that such conversations are a distraction that decrease the team's ability to perform. The leader can then propose a norm around these side conversations. The team uses their decision process to finalize and adopt the norm. If the team does not already have a decision process, then the leader can take the following steps:

1. Ask if there are questions about the proposed norm and address those questions.
2. Ask for builds on the proposed norm and incorporate those builds.
3. Explain that a majority vote will be used to adopt norms.
4. Take a vote on adopting the new team norm.

A second example of a way that a team member experiencing a social needs threat can act out is to make disparaging comments about the team's ability to realize a deliverable. The team leader can use the following team process as an exercise to strengthen their ability to meet a disputed deliverable:

1. The team leader writes the deliverable on a flipchart page or projects the deliverable on a screen for everyone to see.
2. The team leader asks team members to work alone at their seat and come up with realistic barriers to achieving the deliverable. The members are instructed to capture one barrier per

sticky note and generate at least one barrier to achieving the deliverable.

3. The team leader collects the sticky notes with barriers from team members and arranges them in categories on a flipchart page. The leader uses a separate sticky note to label the barrier categories (a sample barrier category might be internal expertise limitations).

4. Team members vote on the barriers most important for the team to address from their perspective in pursuit of that deliverable. A rule of thumb for voting is to divide the total number of barriers, ignoring the categories, by the number of voters and give that number of dots to each team member for voting.

5. The team picks the barriers with the top votes and develops action plans to address them.

There is also the proactive approach of using team process to anticipate and meet the social needs of team members for inclusion and respect, control, and shared understanding. For example, research shows that issue conflict produces a team environment conducive to creativity, whereas people conflict produces an environment that is detrimental to creativity.[22] The team leader can use the following process as an exercise to identify strengths of team members that can be leveraged to maximize the team's performance:

1. The team leader writes down or displays the team's mission for all to see and instructs each team member to think of the gifts or talents that they bring to help achieve the team's mission.

2. Each team member is instructed to capture one to three gifts or talents, one per sticky note, placing a G in the upper-left corner of the sticky note to identify it as a gift. The team leader collects the G sticky notes from members and arranges the gifts in categories on a flipchart page.

3. Each team member is instructed to capture one hook on a sticky note labeled with an *H* in the upper-left corner. The hook is what needs to happen in the team for that member to stay engaged. Again, the team leader collects the *H* sticky notes from members and arranges the hooks in categories on a separate flipchart page.
4. The team reviews the hooks and gifts captured on the flipchart pages and ask questions for clarity and understanding.
5. The team formulates actions to leverage the gifts toward their team mission, including the value of different perspective to ignite creativity, and to realize the hooks.

This section provided tactics for team leaders to address the external leadership challenges of lackluster performance and disruptive behavior by team members. The next section provides tactics for improved team decision-making to address the inherent leadership challenge of faulty thinking.

AVOIDING TEAM LEADERSHIP THINKING TRAPS

A thinking trap is faulty thinking that arises from automatic processing in the nonconscious brain. There is simply too much information at any given point in time for our brain to process using the prefrontal cortex located behind the forehead, which is the seat of logical thought and decision-making. Cognitive biases from the nonconscious are shortcuts used by the brain to direct our attention and filter the incoming stimuli down to what our conscious thinking capacity can handle. Our brain is very good at this. At any given point in time, ten to eleven billion bits of information are coming to the brain from our environment. Fifty of those ten to eleven billion bits can be understood, and up to seven bits, depending on the nature of the information, can be held in short-term memory. Neuroscientist Dr. Arne Dietrich says that "99 percent plus of all the brain's computations occur in the ill-lit basement of the [non]-conscious."[23] And the math works out: fifty of eleven billion is less than half a billionth of a percent. The brain uses the cognitive biases stored in the nonconscious to filter those ten to eleven billion bits of information down to fifty and then down to seven. However, we can miss things that we should have paid attention to, or we can draw the wrong conclusions or assumptions about other people and situations. Much of the time the errors from cognitive biases are inconsequential, but sometimes these errors create barriers to the performance of others. Team leaders do not want to create barriers to the performance of team members whether the creation of these barriers is intentional or not.

A cognitive bias called the bias blind spot is the tendency to see biases in others but not in ourselves. Bias blind spot might be the brain's way of protecting the use of cognitive biases for proper brain functioning. This type of bias makes it very difficult—if not impossible—for a team leader to spot a cognitive bias in themselves that is causing a leadership problem. But the consideration of cognitive biases may help leaders troubleshoot and address a team leadership problem in retrospect.

A primary caveat for team leaders when it comes to thinking traps is in decision-making. Decision-making is particularly vulnerable to faulty thinking from cognitive biases because it can involve taking into account lots of different pieces of information. When there is a lot of information to consider, short-term memory and the prefrontal cortex for high-level thinking can be overwhelmed and automatically tap into the cognitive biases stored in the nonconscious. Fortunately, decision-making by a team can be improved in a number of different ways to help avoid thinking traps.

One tactic to improve team decision-making is to be guided by the values most important to the team's mission. Values can help streamline decision-making by eliminating options that do not align with the team's values. The following team process is a proven way to guide a team to develop values:

1. The team leader writes down or displays the team's mission for everyone to see.
2. Each team member gets a deck of values cards and picks the top ten values from the deck that, from their perspective, are of highest priority to the team's mission.[24] The deck of value cards should include blank cards so team members can handwrite a value they feel is missing.
3. Team members capture their top values on sticky notes, one value per note, and display them on a flipchart page or wall.
4. Team members receive dots for voting; a rule of thumb is to divide the total number of values on the wall by the number of voters or to use five dots. Members use their dots to vote for the values they feel are most important to the team's mission.
5. The team leader selects the top five to seven values based on the voting results.
6. Finally, the team writes a guiding principle for each of the top values using the following format: *We believe [**value**]; therefore, we will [**behavior**]*. The guiding principles are used as a filter to streamline decision-making.

A second tactic to improve team decision-making is to do a blind input exercise for a proposed decision or action that has limited support. This tactic checks that the limited support is not the result of faulty thinking from cognitive biases or social factors that can limit input. The following is a process for a blind input exercise on a proposed decision:

1. The team leader writes down the proposed decision or action for everyone to see.
2. The team leader instructs team members to type up their input on the proposed decision using 12-point Arial type in Word with standard margins. Once everyone is done with their input, they send their input to the same printer.
3. The team leader collects the input from the printer and places the printed pages in the center of the table. Each team member is instructed to select an input page to read aloud.
4. The final step is to go around the room and have each team member read the input they selected from the center of the table. The team needs to consider each piece of input relative to the proposed decision or action to the satisfaction of all members before proceeding to the next piece of input. In this way, multiple perspectives are taken into account to improve the decision-making process.

A third tactic to improve team decision-making is to understand all options regarding a decision as a basis for consensus. A process for this tactic is advocating, as described here:
1. The team leader writes the decision in question on a sticky note as one option. The option is posted on a flipchart page, and the leader asks team members to provide all the alternatives they can think of to that option.
2. Each alternative is captured on a separate note on the same flipchart page.
3. Team members vote for the option they think is best using a checkmark or a dot. Each member gets one vote.
4. The options with no votes are removed from consideration.
5. Each voter gets one minute to advocate for their vote.
6. The final step is a revote. Team members repeat steps 4, 5, and 6 until they reach full consensus on a single option.

A team leader not aware of their internal leadership challenges like lack of skills and experience can inhibit the performance possible from a team. In addition, leaders who don't address problems with lackluster performance and disruptive behavior by team members may face a losing battle for overall team performance. There is also the more subtle challenge of thinking traps that can sabotage decision-making by team leaders.

This chapter provided proven proactive and reactive tactics for team leaders, and, in some cases, for team members to address these team leadership challenges. The next chapter explores the role of members in more detail.

Here are some reflection exercises and questions for this chapter on team leadership to enhance learning:

- Recall a team leadership experience by yourself or by another person that you found disappointing, frustrating, or maddening. Step through the six team leader mindsets relative to that team leadership experience. What mindset(s) could have improved that leadership experience and how?

- Think about a recent time that you experienced negative emotion in a meeting. Which of the three social needs (inclusion and respect, control, shared understanding) could have caused the negative emotion and why?

- Which process tactic(s) most resonated with you, and how would you like to use it?

CHAPTER 4

Troubleshooting Team Composition

The composition of a workplace team is an important factor in team performance independent of other factors such as who the team leader is and how that team operates. Researchers have found that the mere act of forming a team has performance benefits regardless of how different or similar the team members are in appearance and thinking.[1] For example, we like people we perceive to be on our team more than those we perceive to be outside our team. Further, we empathize more with people we perceive to be on our team than with those we perceive to be outside our team. Finally, we are better at inferring the goals, thoughts, and feelings behind the faces of those we consider on our team versus those we consider outside our team. A correlation exists between team performance and the ability of members to infer the thoughts and feelings of one another.[2]

The performance benefits from the mere act of forming a team can be destroyed by incentives for team members to protect self-interest over team interest. For example, a boss who rewards the individual accomplishments of one subordinate with a higher raise than the team contributions of another subordinate is placing more value on self-interest than team interest. I knew individuals with high self-interest at work who took credit for teamwork after the team disbanded. For example, one boss asked me to lead a team to commercialize a new technology. Once the technology was commercialized under my leadership, my boss filed a patent application including all the members except for me. I met with him to inquire about the exclusion, and he explained that I had not contributed to the original idea. My boss did not value my contribution of leading the team that converted the idea to an invention even though converting an idea to an invention is a prerequisite to file a patent application and receive a patent.

Self-interest is wired into our brain's nonconscious networks, but strategic thinking is needed to reconcile self-interest with group interest.[3] Strategic thinking is driven by a compelling vision of the future to achieve long-term results and initiate present actions that otherwise would not be taken. Strategic thinking can produce better results in the long term with good contributions from qualified others. My boss may have succeeded in excluding me from the patent application, but my teamwork skills afforded me career opportunities and promotions while my boss's lack of teamwork skills kept him in the same job until he retired. Fortunately, I understood my teamwork skills were leading to results and so they were strategic to my career in the long term even though I was not getting rewarded for teamwork in the short term.

Team composition problems are difficult to identify and therefore can limit team performance undetected. In contrast, team leadership problems are easy to identify relative to team composition problems. A team leadership problem is identified by the reaction of team members to the leader and vice versa. The quality of the interactions between the team leader and team members provides immediate feedback to identify team leadership problems, but there is no such feedback mechanism to identify a team composition problem. Team composition problems can be confounded by other problems and take time to emerge and effort to identify and rectify.

SYMPTOMS OF TEAM COMPOSITION PROBLEMS

A team composition problem has three basic symptoms. The first symptom is evidence of groupthink. This concept was first described in 1972 as a psychological drive for consensus in group decision-making that suppresses disagreement and prevents the consideration of alternatives.[4] Groupthink is detrimental because it makes a group perform worse working together than an average person could perform working alone.

There are three root causes of groupthink: The first is overconfidence in the group's capabilities, the second is close-mindedness in viewing problems, and the third is strong pressure to conform to a leader's wishes. Groupthink produces defective decision-making because the group fails to examine all alternatives in decision-making and fails to take into account all factors affecting the decision. Groupthink is addressed from a team composition perspective by using proven decision-making processes and by having a mix of team members representing the range of perspectives and experiences needed. Keep in mind that groupthink can also be caused by a team leader who has the positional power or persuasion tactics to pressure members to support the decision that the team leader wants.

A second of three symptoms of a team composition problem is irrational behavior that inhibits the team's ability to achieve the team goal. For example, one team member is against a team decision that helps make progress toward the team's goal, but the member does not provide rationale for their resistance. A member expressing resistance but with no rationale is protecting their own interests or is protecting a third party's interests. A member does not provide a rationale when protecting their own interests because putting your own interests ahead of the team's interests is not socially acceptable. Likewise, a member does not provide a rationale when protecting the interests of a third party because they look weak if members learn they are being manipulated. The team leader needs to assess the cause behind a member's irrational behavior to improve the situation. The cause behind this irrational behavior may also be the behavior of the team leader or another team member.

A third symptom of a team composition problem is poor progress against the team goal. Poor progress can also be caused by leadership and operational problems. But it is related to team composition when there is the wrong number of team members, the wrong mix of members, or the wrong members. Regardless, changing team membership is a reactive approach that is not easy but may be necessary to fix a team composition problem. It is far better to take a strategic approach to team composition from the outset. But using a strategic approach to select team members when the team is formed does not protect you against team composition problems emerging later along the team's journey.

I have been fortunate enough on several occasions to have led a team effort and been empowered to pick the team members. The wise business author Stephen R. Covey speaks to the importance of selecting members when he says, "I am convinced that when recruiting and selecting are done strategically, that is, with long-term thought and proactivity, not based upon the pressure of the moment, it pays enormous long-term dividends."[5] Next, we explore three considerations to practice strategic selection of members: number of members, character and competence criteria, and mix of members.

Large teams are preferred for many reasons. For example, they offer a lot of capabilities through the different skills and unique expertise of the team members. Large teams also offer lots of resources through the assorted relationships and networks of team members and through the various sources of information of members. They also offer input from many different perspectives, which can be helpful for problem solving. Finally, large teams offer a lot of ideas and possible solutions. In fact, team size is a predictor of team innovation.[6]

Small teams are preferred for many reasons.[7] For example, small teams tend to be cohesive because getting to know others on a small team is easy, and therefore trust is easily established. These teams also tend to report high member satisfaction. They also are great for fast decision-making, because consensus can be a faster process with a small group of people than with a large group. Finally, there tends to be more effective individual contribution on a small team compared to a large team so that all team members are engaged in the team's work.

The research findings on the benefits of large teams compared to small teams reveal quite a few trade-offs. For example, research shows it is challenging to have a cohesive team with a lot of capabilities and resources. Also, if you want a team that will generate a lot of different ideas, then chances are the team members will not be satisfied with the team experience. Also, somewhat ironically, if you want a team that will provide a lot of input in team meetings, then chances are the members will not be very engaged outside of meetings. This research points to the team composition challenge of selecting the right number of members to best accomplish a team goal.

The research on team size also raises the question: is there an optimal team size? In 1970, J. Richard Hackman and Neil Vidmar set out to find the perfect team size in a study that asked teams large and small to do several different tasks.[8] Afterward, they asked the participants how strongly they agreed with two statements:

- Their group was too small for the task.
- Their group was too large for the task.

The optimum number of team members from this research was 4.6. But this optimal team size of 4.6 is based on the satisfaction of members with how size related to accomplishing a group task. Recall that member satisfaction was one of the benefits of small teams.

Rich Karlgaard and Michael Malone propose that the optimum team size is 7 plus or minus 2 (7 ± 2).[9] They base this proposal on Harvard psychologist George Miller's finding in 1954 that human short-term memory is capable of holding 7 ± 2 items of information. This proposal makes sense given the research finding that high team performance correlates with equal participation across team members. If you can hold 7 ± 2 bits of information in short-term memory, then members can consider everyone's input as long as the team is 7 ± 2 people in size.

However, neuroscientists have found that the number of items you can hold in short-term memory depends on the nature of those items.[10] If those items are single-digit numbers, then it is no problem to hold seven of them in short-term memory. If those items are seven different perspectives on a scientific problem, then they would be much more difficult to hold in short-term memory.

I have three recommendations for deciding team size based on these research studies. First, make the team as large as possible and manage team climate and team processes expertly when a team goal requires high creativity and innovation. If you do not feel the team leader is qualified to manage the team climate and team process expertly, then you can hire a professional facilitator to partner with the leader.[11] For example, creativity guru Dr. Keith Sawyer writes in his book *Group Genius: The Creative Power of Collaboration*, "Using a trained facilitator is essential to good brainstorming; research shows that groups led by a trained facilitator are twice as creative."[12] Second, use 7 ± 2 team members as a rule of thumb when a team goal does not require high creativity. Third, target five team members when team member satisfaction is important.

The final two considerations after number for strategic selection of team members are mix and criteria for character and competence, which are specific to the team goal. For example, if the team goal requires a high level of creativity, then you want a diverse mix of backgrounds, perspectives, and expertise across team members. In addition, competence criteria for members need to fuel the high creativity needed for the team goal. For example, the expertise of members needs to bring different aspects relevant to the team goal or have a structural parallel to the team goal to bring a new but potentially helpful perspective. Also, the character criteria for members need to support the high creativity needed by accommodating the visible and expertise diversity of members. Thus, character criteria need to promote inclusion across the diversity of members. For example, inclusive behavior correlates with people who are open to new experiences, extroverted, and curious to learn about other people. In fact, inclusive behavior is also important to the diverse perspectives needed to avoid groupthink, one of the signature results of a team composition problem.

THE CHALLENGES OF INCLUSION

Inclusion takes effort because of two primary challenges. The first challenge making inclusion difficult is our natural self-interest. The second challenge is that our brains are wired for exclusion.

Ironically, situations requiring inclusion are also those when our natural self-interest takes over. For example, the first sign that someone feels excluded in some way is that person expressing negative emotions, which can lead to silence behavior or violence behavior.[13] A team member who feels excluded by the comments of another member may come across in different ways such as the following:

- The receiving team member gets angry (negative emotion).
- The receiving team member stops contributing to the meeting (silence behavior).
- The receiving team member insults the offending team member (violence behavior).

Our brain is wired to pay attention to negative emotion so that we can determine what another person's negative emotion means for us. But, to be inclusive, you need to make the extra effort to determine what another person's negative emotion means to them. You make this extra effort by practicing the skills of cognitive and emotional empathy.

Cognitive and emotional empathy are skills that can be developed with formal training just like public speaking skills can be developed with formal training.[14] If you are interested in training to develop cognitive and emotional empathy, then I recommend finding a trainer with experience in behavioral skills training. This type of training is a proven method to develop social skills such as cognitive and emotional empathy by providing instructions, modeling effective behaviors, and practicing with feedback.[15]

Emotional empathy is the ability to feel what another person feels based on assessing the situation and observing the person's behavior and facial expressions. False consensus effect is a nonconscious bias from our brain that can get in the way of developing emotional empathy. It is the tendency to assume that other people feel, think, and believe the same as we do.

Cognitive empathy is the ability to imagine how we would feel in another person's position based on a hypothetical model in our mind that takes into account the situation. Out-group bias can get in the way of developing cognitive empathy. This type of bias is the tendency to have negative views about people you view as outside of your group in a given situation. Stereotypes, or associations between how you categorize a person with a particular trait, also can get in the way of developing cognitive empathy.

Emotional and cognitive empathy come easier to some people than other people just like public speaking comes easier to some people than other people. You improve public speaking skills by doing public speaking and getting objective feedback on what you did well and on what you need to do different or better. You learn from the feedback and change your approach to public speaking for the next time so you can do a better job. Likewise, you improve emotional and cognitive empathy by trying to figure out what others are thinking and feeling and then asking the other person whether your interpretation is accurate. You learn from how accurate your interpretation is and change your approach to emotional and cognitive empathy for the next time to be more accurate.

Another challenge to inclusion is that our brains are wired for exclusion. We all carry implicit stereotypes in our nonconscious brain that cause us to exclude others. Implicit stereotypes are associations between a people category and a particular trait assigned to that category which we are not aware of because they are stored in our nonconscious brain.[16] An example of an implicit stereotype is men are good at math. The people category is gender, specifically men, and the trait is math skill. This stereotype would be implicit if we are not aware that the stereotype exists in our nonconscious brain. The challenge is we all have a bias blind spot, which is the tendency to see biases in other people but not in ourselves. Bias blind spot is one of the reasons that nonconscious-bias training is ineffective.

In 2019, the *New York Times* published an article about Julie Sweet, the chief executive for Accenture North America, a consulting firm with 469,000 employees and annual revenues of

$17.8 billion. In the article, Julie recalls her first experience with gender diversity training in 1999, which occurred just two weeks before a meeting in which she would be elected as partner. Julie points out that she was the most senior woman in the room but still in the minority compared to the number of men. The facilitator of the nonconscious-bias training illustrated some different barriers to leadership and then turned to Julie to share her experience. Julie responds as follows according to the article: "To this day, I remember I went to speak, and I started sobbing. I could not speak. I couldn't compose myself, and I left. I went back to my office."[17]

Bias blind spot is why nonconscious-bias training designed to raise awareness for gender diversity leads to disdainful female leaders and confused male leaders. Female leaders are upset because they are still in the minority in their ranks and they recognize the implicit biases of others that are holding them back. Male leaders are confused because they don't recognize the implicit biases in themselves that are holding back female leaders. Nonconscious-bias training is one example of how awareness of implicit biases is not enough to produce the new behaviors needed to eliminate performance barriers present in a diverse workforce. Bias blind spot is a built-in brain filter that prevents inclusion.

Practicing inclusion is hard, but diversity is more complex than we realize. For example, some cultures tend to process the environment more analytically, focusing on smaller details and viewing things from a more rules-based perspective. But other cultures tend to process the environment more holistically, seeing broader patterns and tapping into more intuitive thinking.[18] An analytical, rules-based perspective or a holistic, intuitive perspective taken alone will miss content that could be important to a problem or an opportunity. Further, other considerations for social behavior are a subset of culture, such as country of origin, socioeconomic class, degree of education, religious practices, family history, race, and gender. For example, actress Thandie Newton said in her TED (Technology, Entertainment, Design) talk: "There's actually more genetic difference between a black Kenyan and a black Ugandan than there is between a black Kenyan and a white Norwegian."[19] In other words, the ways in which we are different are not necessarily predictable by visible differences like the color of one's skin.

An alternative to the losing battle of expecting inclusive behavior is to do a regular inventory of your workplace interactions to identify inclusivity challenges. An inclusivity challenge is a barrier to workplace performance caused when you or another person feels excluded. It appears as a bad, awkward, or disappointing interaction in the workplace. To identify an inclusivity challenge, first reflect on your workplace interactions over the past week and list the ones that felt bad, strange, or below your expectations in some way. Next, for each poor interaction, answer the following questions, being as specific as possible:

- Does your poor interaction involve a gender, racial, age, or cultural minority situation?
- Does your poor interaction involve a gender, racial, age, or cultural difference being salient in some way such as through behavior or appearance?
- Did your poor interaction involve negative emotion? If so, then what negative emotions and by whom?
- Did your poor interaction involve silence or violence behaviors? If so, then what specific silence behaviors (i.e., passive aggression, sarcasm, avoidance, or withdrawal) and violence behaviors (i.e., control, name calling, or verbal attacks) and by whom?

If you answered yes to any of these questions for a given poor interaction, then you have identified an inclusivity challenge. The next two steps help identify the root cause behind this challenge.

The first step to understanding the cause behind an inclusion problem is to identify which social needs could have been affected for you or the other person during the interaction. I use the five social need categories that have been identified by the NeuroLeadership Institute: status, certainty, autonomy, relatedness, and fairness.[20] Research shows that the human brain has a need for status in a social situation because this increases our likelihood of survival. Similarly, the human brain has a need for certainty, autonomy, relatedness, and fairness in social situations because of the potential negative and positive impacts on our survival. Consider which of these social needs may have been decreased for you or for the other person during the interaction.

The second step to understanding the cause behind an inclusivity challenge is to identify which implicit biases could have been involved during the interaction.[21] Some similarity biases are driven by our need to see others whom we perceive as similar to us as good and trustworthy. Other experience biases are driven by our belief that what we sense to be real for ourselves is real for others. Some expedience biases are driven by our need to simplify the processing of a lot of information. For example, some distance biases are driven by our tendency to assign greater value to things that are in closer proximity according to time, space, responsibility, and impact. Finally, some safety biases are driven by our tendency to assign greater value to losing something over gaining something. The aim of this step is to determine if similarity, experience, expedience, distance, or safety biases could have played a role in causing the inclusion problem. Similarity biases tend to play a role when a gender, racial, or cultural difference or a minority situation is involved in the inclusivity challenge.

When you gain some insight into the possible causes of your inclusivity challenge, you can research a behavioral tactic that could have improved the situation. It may be too late to apply this tactic to the particular interaction, but you can try it next time. For example, the type of behavioral tactic to try for an inclusivity challenge that involves a similarity bias is a way to discover that a person we perceive to be different from us has similarities to us. In other words, you address a bias with a tactic that removes the bias. To address an experience bias, you need a tactic that uncovers how an experience is different for another person. Similarly, to address an expedience bias, you need a tactic for a more deliberate assessment of a lot of information. Finally, for a distance bias, you need a tactic to remove the distance, and for a safety bias, you need a tactic to also consider what can be gained.

I will apply this reflective process to address an inclusivity challenge that an anonymous professional shared with me: a woman is nominated to an organization's Leadership Development Program (LDP) by her male boss. The woman's boss needs to inform her of the nomination because the woman has been selected to participate in the prestigious leadership program. Every year, about twenty-five people are nominated to LDP, but only eight people are selected to participate in the program. The boss tells the woman about the nomination, and the woman says, "I'm pregnant. How will that impact my nomination?" The boss freezes, which is a form of silence behavior. The boss may have had this reaction because of a perceived status threat. For example, the boss may have worried about saying the wrong thing and looking like a bad manager or getting in trouble with his manager, which are damaging to his status. The boss could have experienced a distance bias because he was surprised about the employee's situation, so he reacted to avoid the situation. A behavioral tactic when experiencing a distance bias is to remove the distance. In this case, the boss could have imagined that the female subordinate was a friend with a health issue to remove the distance. The boss would have produced a supportive and appropriate response by imagining that the subordinate was a friend in a challenging professional situation. The boss can remember his sensitivity to difference and try this tactic the next time a subordinate says something that causes him to freeze.

LEVERAGING THE DIVERSITY OF TEAM MEMBERS

Teams need to walk a tightrope when it comes to diversity. They want enough diversity of perspective to have the expertise and knowledge to solve problems and pursue opportunities related to their mission. But too much diversity of perspective can break down communication and trust when people don't understand each other. A lack of trust is a real problem for team performance.

Each team member should strive to have a positive balance in the trust account with each other member for optimal performance. Trust is at the heart of the shared understanding, respect, inclusion, and autonomy needed to support high team performance. Saying something or doing something that makes a member experience a positive feeling makes a deposit in the trust account. Positive emotion is our brain's way of acknowledging that an interaction has been rewarding in some way, so we will be driven to interact more with that person. In contrast, saying or doing something that makes a member experience a negative feeling makes a withdrawal from the trust account. Negative emotion is our brain's way of signaling that an interaction has been threatening in some way, so we will be cautious in future interactions with that person. The higher the balance in the trust account with a team member, the higher the trust with that person. In fact, scientists find that a ratio of three to one positive emotional experiences to negative emotional experiences over time predicts whether a person will thrive rather than languish.[22]

In my first staff meeting with a new vice president (VP) of a product innovation group, the VP said to me: "I disagreed with

'Fred' on forming the group you are leading." This was the first withdrawal from our trust account because I had high respect for this VP's predecessor, "Fred," and this comment made me angry. Later in the meeting, the new VP said to me: "I don't understand the value your group delivers, and there is no way to measure it." This was the second withdrawal from our trust account because the VP chose to criticize my group rather than help improve my group's contribution, which made me feel excluded. The new VP made no deposits in our trust account in that first staff meeting but continued to ignite more negative emotional experiences than positive emotional experiences for me in our interactions, which kept the balance in our trust account negative. I did not trust the new VP, and I doubt he trusted me either. The only good news is that the poor relationship with the new VP contributed to my decision to look for and find a better opportunity elsewhere in the organization.

A tactic for building trust among team members is conscious inclusion. Some may take the benefits of inclusion for granted because they have not experienced social exclusion. Empirical research has revealed much about the damaging cognitive and health impacts of this type of exclusion.[23]

Conscious inclusion is a proactive way to make deposits in the trust account with another person and get around the brain's nonconscious tendency for exclusion. You make deposits in the trust account with a team member by addressing the social needs of that person. For the social need of respect, a team member can make a trust deposit by helping another member feel respected and valued as part of the group. For the social need of autonomy, a member can make a trust deposit by ensuring another member has opportunities to contribute and is fairly recognized for their contributions. A team can also implement processes to ensure that every member is asked to contribute, opportunities are shared across members, and everyone receives credit for their contributions. For the social need of belonging, a member can make a trust deposit by being kind and courteous toward another member. Other ways a team member can make trust deposits for inclusion are showing genuine interest in another member and finding shared experiences with that person. A team can also schedule social events and design team exercises to help members get to know one another to promote inclusion. Finally, for the social need of shared understanding, a member can make a trust deposit by informing another member of things impacting their work they didn't already know about.

Implicit stereotypes from diversity are a source of error in team decision-making, just as faulty thinking from automatic processing in our nonconscious brain is a concern for team leaders in decision-making. There are several tactics to leverage team diversity for improved decision-making.

One tactic to leverage team diversity in decision-making is structuring team decision-making according to roles for different types of decisions. Structuring team decision-making is particularly important when decisions impacting the team can happen both inside and outside the team. RACI analysis is a tactic for gaining role clarity in decision-making. RACI—an acronym for Responsible, Accountable, Consult, and Inform—represents the different roles that people play in decision-making.

In RACI, responsibility can be shared, whereas accountability cannot. As a result, more than one person cannot be accountable for a given decision. Accountability is specific to an individual and the results expected of that individual in the workplace, whereas responsibility is a person's commitment to a team goal or a team task. The person accountable to a decision has veto power while the people responsible for the decision do not. Consult in RACI analysis is for the people who need to have input to a decision but are not responsible or accountable for the decision. Inform in RACI analysis is for the people who need to know about the decision after it is made. The team leader can draft an RACI matrix listing the types of decisions that impact the team as rows and shows the people responsible, accountable, consulted, and informed for each type of decision in columns. The leader reviews the draft RACI matrix with the team for input. The final RACI matrix is used as a guide for team decision-making.

Another tactic to leverage team diversity for improved decision-making is to use a structured process. For example, the team leader writes down or displays a decision that the team needs to make for all team members to see. The leader can ask if there are questions for clarity on the decision and then revise the decision as agreed by the team. The leader can also ask if alternatives to the decision need to be considered. If alternatives are identified, then the team needs to select which version of the decision to discuss first. Finally, the leader decides whether full consensus is needed for the selected decision or if a majority vote will suffice. The leader needs to take into account that a full consensus process takes considerable more time than a majority vote, so the impact of the decision must warrant the extra time needed for full consensus.

Sometimes a team is too big to walk the tightrope of leveraging diversity and making forward progress. When you have a large but engaged team, an effective tactic is to create a subteam structure. Subteams can be aligned with team goals or key team activities. The team leader drafts charters for each subteam and then asks for input from the team to finalize their charters. The leader can appoint subteam leaders or ask for volunteers to submit their names offline for consideration. The leader selects subteam leaders based on the character and competence requirements for leadership of the new teams. Remaining team members can volunteer to participate in a subteam by approaching the respective leader, or subteam leaders can recruit members within or outside the existing team. The large team then becomes a steering committee for the work of the subteams. Each subteam leader provides a status update of their subteam's work at steering committee meetings and responds to questions, concerns, and input from remaining steering committee members. Steering committee members are responsible for assuring that the work of the subteams supports the original goals and objectives and is conducted in a high-quality and efficient manner.

So far we have discussed the team composition challenges of selecting the right number of team members, the right mix of members, and members with the traits needed. Diversity is needed in teamwork to avoid the problem of groupthink and to maximize performance on tough group tasks. The challenges of diversity include addressing unintended misunderstandings and the natural tendency to exclude those different from us. Now we turn to problematic behaviors by team members caused by external influences.

UNSHACKLING TEAM MEMBERS FROM EXTERNAL INFLUENCES

What happens outside a team can impact team performance. For example, there are different forms of external pressure on performance. In organizations, a team's performance can be judged by the team leader's boss, team members' bosses, an executive who is sponsoring the team, and executives whose organizations are impacted by the team's work. The team can put their best foot forward by providing input to the people outside the team who are most likely to judge the performance early in the team's existence. Specifically, the team can develop a status update process that meets their needs of the team and of those judging the performance. This process gives a team the opportunity to tout their accomplishments and seek support for setbacks as needed. It also gives them autonomy to work alone between status updates. The following procedure can be used as a guideline to develop a status update process.

TEAM PROCESS FOR STATUS UPDATES

1. The team decides who needs to receive status updates on their progress toward goals and objectives. The people who are to receive these updates (the judgers) are those in a position to judge the team's performance and influence others about the performance.

2. The team drafts a status update schedule based on logical milestones from their goals and objectives. This schedule shows each milestone and the date that the milestone is to be completed. One or more of these milestones can be presented as a go or no-go decision to give the judger an opportunity for input if appropriate. The milestones need to be measurable by the team. The more quantitative the milestones can be, the more appealing that status update will be to judgers who tend to be micromanagers.

3. After the team finalizes the content and schedule of the status update, they can create a template to fill in for each status update. The template describes the milestone and has space for accomplishments and concerns relevant to the milestone. The template can include a stoplight with a color code: for example, green if the milestone has been accomplished on time, yellow if there are concerns, and red if the milestone needs to be changed. Although the color code for stoplights is fairly well understood, the template should include an explanation of the color code for clarity.

4. The team or the team leader sets up a meeting with each judger to review the draft update schedule and status update template. The team or leader can meet with judgers one at a time or as a group. Input on the status update schedule and template from the judgers is incorporated during the meeting as appropriate. Input on the status

update schedule and template from the judgers that needs more thought is captured as a follow-up item.

5. The team discusses the input from the judgers that needs more thought and produces a final version of the status update schedule and template. The final versions of the schedule and template are sent to the judgers and the update process begins.

Another form of external pressure on team performance is a decrease in the team's budget. For example, a top-down cost-cutting program can result in cutting team budgets across the organization. In this case, a team needs to adopt a cost-conscious approach to their work. It can be argued that a team should always take a cost-conscious approach to get the most out of every dollar they spend, but this is a case when a team needs to adjust their work for a lower budget than planned. The team can take the following steps to prioritize their goals and chart a path forward consistent with a new lower budget.

TEAM PROCESS TO ADJUST WORK
FOR A NEW LOWER BUDGET

1. The team writes their goals, objectives, and strategies on sticky notes, one per note.
2. The team works together to place each sticky note in the appropriate quadrant of a two-by-two matrix drawn on a flipchart. The upper-right quadrant is for goals, objectives, and strategies that if met will bring high value or benefit to the organization and to which at least half the team members must contribute. The upper-left quadrant is for goals, objectives, and strategies that if met will bring

high value or benefit to the organization and to which less than half the members must contribute. The lower-right quadrant is for goals, objectives, and strategies that if met will bring low to medium value or benefit to the organization and to which at least half the members must contribute. The lower-left quadrant is for goals, objectives, and strategies that if met will bring low to medium value or benefit to the organization and to which less than half the members must contribute. The team is not creating a plot, so the position of the sticky note in a quadrant does not matter. Also, there can be no notes straddling quadrants.

3. The team brainstorms ways to achieve the goals, objectives, and strategies in the upper-right quadrant within the new lower budget. All ideas are captured. An action item is generated to process the ideas and create a new budget plan for review and discussion by the team.

4. The team can explore if the goals, objectives, and strategies in the upper-left quadrant may be accomplished through other ways. All ideas are captured. A separate action item is generated to process these ideas into recommendations for review and discussion by the team.

5. The team's milestones and schedule may also need to be updated as a result of the prioritization exercise and new budget plan.

6. The goals, objectives, and strategies in the remaining two quadrants can be revisited if some budget is left over or if new funds become available to the team.

A team's budget can be cut by an executive who is not happy with the team's performance. In this case, the team or the team leader needs to meet with the unhappy executive to understand the performance problem from the executive's perspective. After this meeting, the team can discuss what they learned and how to address the performance problem. The team might consider a go or no-go milestone approach. That is, the budget would be reevaluated after each go or no-go milestone. This approach gives the team an opportunity to gain back the support of the executive by delivering agreed-to results on time and on budget.

Team performance can be limited when a team has a laser focus on results. For example, external influences play a role when a team charged with a change initiative has team members from the parts of the organization most impacted by the initiative. It is not uncommon for bosses of members representing groups impacted by the change in a negative way to be resistant to that change and put pressure on their subordinates to also resist it. The most effective way to confront resistance to change is to follow a proven process for change management. Such a process provides a safe and effective way to identify and address valid resistance to a change initiative. A change management process helps free members from unwanted resistance from bosses concerned with the change initiative because the process considers all concerns. If the team leader is not trained in change management, then a member can recommend that the team invest in change management training for one or more of their members. If the leader is trained in change management, then the leader needs to design a process for the team to implement the change management approach. Several proven approaches to change management are available, such as ADKAR,[24] the Kotter eight-step process for leading change,[25] Fujitsu's Macroscope methodology,[26] and others.

A final example of how working on a team with a laser focus on results can limit team performance is the work of other teams overlapping with or impacting the team's work. A team paying attention only to their results can miss opportunities from working with others. For example, a corporate team I was leading decided to initiate a project on an environmental assessment method for products. Our team saw value in coordinating the individual efforts across different business units to develop shared resources and practices to benefit the organization's customers. Unfortunately, the people doing the environmental assessments for products were not impressed with our coordination effort idea. I was participating in regular updates with an overseas colleague who was a member of a similar corporate team. The overseas team was higher ranking than my team, which is why my coordination was with a member of that team. My overseas colleague put me in touch with individuals in his country who were also involved in the same type of environmental assessment. It turned out that the real value in coordinating the environmental assessment efforts between countries was sharing databases. This opportunity would not have been identified if I had not established a coordination effort with a similar team in another country. Teams need to identify other teams in the organization working on similar goals and whose goals impact their team's goals so coordination efforts can be pursued.

A team pursues a coordination effort with another team through the team leaders of the two respective teams. The two leaders set up a meeting to assess the potential impacts of the other team's work on their own team. Even if one team is higher ranking, the lower-ranking leader can request a meeting with the higher-ranking leader to explore opportunities for coordination and collaboration. The agenda for the meeting between the two leaders would begin with each leader sharing the goals, objectives, and strategies for their team. Next, the leaders would discuss concerns and opportunities for coordination and collaboration. Finally, they would schedule a follow-up meeting to bring back specific recommendations and proposed actions from their respective teams based on the things learned in this initial meeting.

If a higher-ranking team leader says no to a meeting requested by a lower-ranking leader and does not provide an alternative contact, then the lower-ranking leader needs to take a different approach. The lower-ranking leader can work with their team to draft a list of questions to assess the impact of the other team's work on their work. This leader next brings the questions to their boss or to an executive sponsor of their team for input. If one of those two people can't answer the questions, then the boss or team sponsor can use their network and influence to answer the questions. If the boss or executive sponsor still can't answer the questions, then the leader, together with the boss or executive sponsor, needs to assess the situation. The leader and boss or executive sponsor may decide if it would be better to suspend the team's work until the results and impacts of the other team's work are known.

External influences on team members may cause a member to leave a team. For example, I had a strong member who found a better career opportunity at another company. This member was leaving the company, so they had to leave my team too. External influences can also cause needed changes to team composition, such as the need for different expertise than that represented by existing members. For example, a change in marketing strategy may impact the type of expertise needed on a team compared to the existing expertise on the team. The next section provides tactics for changing team membership.

FIXING TEAM MEMBERSHIP PROBLEMS

Research shows that leaders who focus on both people and goals get the best results.[27] Likewise, teams that focus on both team members and goals will get the best results. Members are the most important resource for a team to accomplish its goals. Sometimes great care and strategic consideration go into selecting members and sometimes not. Sometimes members are appointed, and sometimes the team leader gets to select the members. Regardless of how members are selected, predicting a team's journey can be hard at the outset. A team evolves over time in response to member input, external factors, and elected changes in direction. The members who kick off a team effort may not be the same members needed as the team evolves.

A decision to change team membership should not be taken lightly since it disrupts the existing team dynamics and introduces new challenges the team may need to overcome. For example, what worked before the change in team membership for decision-making or collecting input may need to be modified to accommodate the needs of new team members. New members may bring behaviors that decrease productivity, which could necessitate new processes or norms to regain productivity. Also, losing a member might leave an important gap in expertise or external resources that needs to be filled. Furthermore, a decision to change team membership often starts with the need to remove one or more members to accommodate new needs. The decision to remove one or more members is perhaps the most challenging type of team membership change. A good departure process for members will help minimize disruption and address unanticipated challenges. The departure process should be established before team membership changes are needed.

A thoughtful departure process is important for several reasons. A good departure process is helpful for recruiting new team members in the future, preserving a good team reputation, and keeping remaining members motivated and engaged. For example, a former member who is disgruntled by a poor departure process may say bad things about the team that will damage the team's reputation and hamper recruitment efforts. A good departure process needs to start with a reason that both the team and the member can accept and feel justified for parting ways. For example, it is not enough to say that a member's behavior is disruptive. The reason for parting ways needs to identify the cause of the disruptive behavior in a way that shows why the transition will be good for both the member and the team. Here are some sample justifiable reasons to initiate a departure process for a member:

- The team member does not have access to resources that the team needs while someone else who will be recruited in their place does have access. Parting ways will remove the member from a frustrating situation and help streamline the team's work.

- The team's goal works against the team member's boss's wishes. Parting ways will eliminate this conflict of interest for the member and improve the team's productivity.

- The team member's expertise, while valuable to the organization, does not have relevance to the current problems and opportunities the team is facing. Parting ways will enable the member to apply their expertise where needed elsewhere in the organization. Parting ways will also enable the team to recruit a new member with the expertise needed at this point in the team's journey.

A team's departure process might include a way for team members to express appreciation for the time and effort the departing member put in as part of the team. There are a number of different ways to appreciate a departing member. For example, appreciation for the departing member can be expressed in a private meeting between the team leader, the member, and the member's boss. Appreciation for the departing member can also be expressed in a meeting with the entire team, and the member's boss could be invited to attend that meeting. Appreciation for the departing member can also be expressed with a card signed by all members or in an email.

A main point of a team's departure process is to bring closure to the departing team member and to the remaining members. Closure for a transition in team membership can be achieved in a number of different ways: for example, a lunch or office party to thank the departing member for their participation. Alternatively, the team might hold a meeting in which a parting gift that includes a team logo or picture is presented to the departing member as a way to commemorate their team experience.

A team not only needs to develop a departure process before changes in team membership are needed but also needs to develop an onboarding process. A good onboarding process helps a new team member establish group identity. Onboarding also helps a new member get up to speed as quickly as possible so they can contribute to the team as soon as possible. Team onboarding can be modeled after human resource practices for onboarding new employees. For example, regarding onboarding new employees: "Onboarding is the process of integrating a new employee with a company and its culture, as well as getting a new hire the tools and information needed to become a productive member of the team."[28] This definition of onboarding a new employee for an organization can be applied to onboarding a new member.

When I was chairperson of the Corporate Sustainability Community Council (CSCC), I kept a file of documents for new members. The documents were those that a new member of the CSCC would need to review to be able to understand the status of our work, how we work, and our mission and goals. The file of documents for new members was an "evergreen" file because as the team evolved, what a new member of the team would need to know and understand to contribute evolved too. So an important part of the onboarding process is a document management process and system. Document management is needed to review the onboarding documents and ensure they are still the most relevant and important documents at a given point in time in the team's journey.

I think an important part of team onboarding is a one-on-one meeting between the team leader and new team member to discuss the team's charter, culture, and norms—whether documented or not (although onboarding is made easier if these items are documented). If a recruitment process was used in the initial formation of the team, then this same recruitment process can be used in onboarding before the new member's first meeting. For example, for the CSCC, the assignment for the first meeting was to produce a drawing that told the story of why sustainability was important to members either personally or professionally. This assignment became part of CSCC's onboarding process and also showed our tolerance to a wide range of artistic expression.

Team members are a primary resource for performance. If members are not selected with care, then they can become a liability to performance. This chapter provided tactics for a strategic selection of members as well as guidance for onboarding and offboarding members to accommodate needed and unanticipated changes in team membership. The chapter also provided tools for leveraging diversity on a team to counteract our natural tendency to exclude those we perceive as different. Finally, the chapter also discussed tactics to address team performance problems caused by external influences on members. The next chapter will look at the influence of team climate on performance.

Here are some reflection exercises and questions for this chapter on team composition to enhance learning:

- What aspects of troubleshooting team composition most resonated with you and why?

- Recall a positive team experience. What about the composition of the team and team members made the team work so well?
- In what ways can you identify and address inclusivity challenges in your workplace?

CHAPTER 5

Troubleshooting Team Climate

Team climate, the environment that team members experience in meetings, is inviting or uninviting just like a room is inviting or uninviting. Team climate is made up of different components like a room's climate is made up of different components. For example, I am sensitive to temperature in determining room comfort, whereas my husband is sensitive to the type of furniture in the room. In fact, my husband would say that my comfort zone for temperature is impossibly narrow. For teams, I am sensitive to how a team leader behaves in determining comfort, whereas my husband is sensitive to how floor time is distributed. My husband is a professor, so he expects adequate floor time whether he is in the office or at home.

Team climate can drive efficiency and effectiveness in team meetings or be a barrier to group performance. I am far more productive working in an air-conditioned office on a hot and sticky summer day than working outside where all I can think about is the beads of sweat coalescing all over my body. Similarly, a team that practices a constructive debate of issues will perform better than a team whose disagreements escalate to personal conflicts that make emotions run high.

The team leader tends to have a disproportionate influence on team climate because the leader initiates and shapes the climate at every meeting. But team climate is the sum total of individual team member behaviors even though the leader has a big influence. The host of a party can ask you to take off your shoes at the front door, and you can decide to have a good time anyway or sulk because you don't get to show off your new shoes. A team leader can shoot down your idea for no good reason, and you can decide to stay engaged anyway or withdraw from the meeting. Not all leader and member behaviors are created equal though. Leader and member behaviors can galvanize engagement by others or can discourage engagement by others. A good team climate is characterized by equal participation across members on average.[1]

Equal participation across team members is easier said than done. If you have equal participation, then you have succeeded in all members feeling comfortable enough to contribute to the team task at hand. But different people have different preferences when it comes to the team climate that promotes their best work and involvement in a meeting. It is not enough for a team leader or a member to pay attention to the climate elements that make them feel comfortable to participate in a team. A leader and members need to be aware of the symptoms that team climate problems exist for other members.

SYMPTOMS OF TEAM CLIMATE PROBLEMS

Team climate problems occur when the environment of a team meeting gets in the way of a member's participation. I have experienced many team climate problems over the course of my corporate career. For example, while at a premier global chemicals and life sciences company, I remember being invited to a meeting of research and development (R&D) managers with the global head of R&D from Europe. The meeting objective was for the R&D managers to understand how our work supported the global R&D strategy. I thought it was important to understand everything the global head of R&D said because he did not travel to the United States very often, so I took copious notes. My method to understand what someone is saying to me is to take notes—"from the hand to the mind" as the saying goes. But midsentence, the global head of R&D looked directly at me and asked why I was taking notes. I explained that this was my way of processing what he was saying. He said that what he was saying was company confidential and was not to be shared outside of the room. I assured him that I was using a personal notebook for my use only. The damage had been done, however; I sensed his mistrust and stopped taking notes as my will to understand his message evaporated. So the things we say and do in a group can impact the ability of others to stay engaged and be productive.

One symptom of a team climate problem is nonproductive conflict, which can take different forms. One form of nonproductive conflict is personal conflict between team members, which researchers have shown is damaging to creativity and problem solving.[2] Another form is passive-aggressive behavior, which researchers have shown can lead to a downward escalatory spiral of negative emotion between two people.[3] This is like sitting in a hot room next to a window channeling the sun onto your already sweaty face. Passive-aggressive behavior is indirect conflict like pretending to pay attention to someone you are angry with or agreeing to an action you have no intention of completing. Many people are good at picking up on passive-aggressive behavior and will call the other person out on their behavior. The person with the passive aggression will deny the accusation, which will make the accuser more angry and frustrated. The increasing spiral of negative emotion triggered by the passive-aggressive behavior will not produce a productive outcome. Moderate and high levels of negative emotion are also damaging to creativity and problem solving.[4]

Whereas nonproductive conflict is a symptom of a team climate problem, some types of conflict enhance team performance. For example, idea debate has been found to correlate with a team's creativity and ability to innovate. Also, correcting another team member's mistake in the spirit of learning and improving is also important to creativity in teams.[5]

A second symptom of a team climate problem is low tolerance to the creativity needed for problem solving and opportunity identification. Team members with a low tolerance for uncertainty can see creativity as disruptive, but the right level of uncertainty in the form of thoughtful risk taking and openness to change correlates with improved problem solving and opportunity identification by groups.[6] Several creativity researchers have shown the importance of the right climate to creativity. For example, one researcher found that creativity in the workplace correlates with your genuine feelings and attitudes about your work life.[7] Specifically, the more meaningful your work is to you, the more positive your emotions, and the more positive your perceptions of your coworkers, the more likely you are to be creative at work. The pinnacle of my corporate career was serving as head of sustainability reporting to the CEO because of the creativity unleashed from working on a cause so meaningful to me. Another researcher found that group climate for optimum creativity needs to support focus on a problem, confidence in addressing the problem, motivation to solve the problem, and the ability to access diverse perspectives.[8] For example, fear of saying something wrong disrupts your focus on a problem, destroys your confidence in addressing a problem, diminishes your motivation to solve the problem, and prevents access to your unique perspective by fellow team members.

A third symptom of a team climate problem is relying on team building to generate a high-performance team climate. Team building is a technique to help team members get comfortable working with one another, but a healthy team climate requires a balance of autonomy and collaboration. I remember being on a team in which the team leader would lead the team through elaborate team-building exercises. One exercise was a role play on a deserted island, and because we got so involved in the role play, there was no time left to address the team agenda. We did a lot of fun team-building exercises on that team but always fell behind on the agenda. While the team building was fun, it was a distraction from the work needed to fuel high-performance teamwork.

The symptoms of team climate problems illustrate the balancing act required to build a high-performance team climate like my narrow temperature range to be comfortable in a room. For example, the symptom of nonproductive conflict shows that a healthy climate balances productive conflict with agreement. Specifically, team members don't always need to agree, but when they disagree, they need to engage in the types of conflict helpful to performance and avoid the types of conflict damaging to performance. The second symptom of low tolerance to creativity illustrates the importance of balancing certainty and uncertainty. Certainty is needed after different options have been vetted by a team to set a direction or begin a project implementation while tolerance to uncertainty is needed in the early stages of problem solving and opportunity identification. Finally, the third symptom of overreliance on team building is about balance between having fun and doing the work. Fun is an important ingredient in meeting social needs like relatedness and fairness, and fun supports the climate needed for creativity. But too much fun gets in the way of the individual work that fuels creativity and produces the results that the team is committed to deliver.

Team climate that is conducive to high performance needs to strike the right balance between contrasting behaviors like productive conflict and agreement, certainty and uncertainty, and fun and work. But team climate also needs to address the individual preferences of team members when it comes to conflict, uncertainty, and fun. Researchers have found that the most creative individuals also strike a balance between contrasting behaviors.[9] For example, highly creative individuals express contrasting personality traits like high introspection and high awareness of the external environment at different times.[10] The key to a good team climate is managing the balance of contrasting behaviors needed within the comfort zone of members. The first step to achieving a good team climate is identifying problems with the team climate.

WAYS TO IDENTIFY TEAM CLIMATE PROBLEMS

A shortcoming in team performance due to team climate is hard to detect, and the symptoms of team climate problems do not point to solutions. You can, however, survey team members to test for specific problems with team climate. Members are experiencing the team climate and are in the best position to identify problems with it.

A team can perform a team climate health check at a team meeting to assess how supportive or limiting the current team climate is to the team's performance. A simple team climate health check can be designed around the three indications of a toxic work climate.[11] For example, the team leader can create a handout with the following information:

- Rate on a scale of 1 (none or low) to 5 (high) the level of emotional well-being and satisfaction you experience in team meetings on average. Please explain.

- Rate on a scale of 1 (none or low) to 5 (high) your contribution to the team's goals and objectives in team meetings on average. Please explain.
- Rate on a scale of 1 (none or low) to 5 (high) the helpfulness of your behaviors inside and outside of team meetings toward achieving team goals and objectives on average. Please explain.

The team leader can anchor the ranking scale for each statement on the team climate health check as follows: 1 means none or low, 2 means lower than average, 3 means average, 4 means higher than average, and 5 means high. The leader processes the rankings inside the current meeting for immediate discussion or outside the meeting for discussion at a later time. Individual rankings of 3 and lower indicate problems with the current team climate and opportunities for improvement based on further climate assessment. Comments, if provided, can help identify the specific problems that need to be addressed to improve team climate for team members.

Team climate is assessed by studying changes in the variables that characterize a team's environment over time. Three types of variables characterize team climate and can be remembered with the acronym SOS: the first S is for structural variables, the O is for outside influences, and the second S is for social variables. Examples of structural variables are team processes, procedures, guidelines, size, leadership effectiveness, and logistics. Examples of outside influences are the work of other teams impacting the team goal, trends impacting the team goal, and external influences on team member behaviors. Finally, examples of social variables are team interactions, member emotional intelligence, and member empathy skills. A team climate assessment based on SOS is available for download (*https://fulcrumconnection.com/blog/posts/team-climate-assessment/*, password is *sOstca2021*). Other team climate surveys are available also, such as the Situational Outlook Questionnaire by the Creative Problem Solving Group.[12]

If problem solving and innovation are important to your team's goals and objectives, then you can perform a simple climate assessment focused on ways to nurture creativity. This team creativity assessment is based on the creative platform,[13] a model based on researching the conditions needed to enhance creativity in workplace teams. The team leader can create a handout with the following information:

- Rate on a scale of 1 (none or low) to 5 (high) your level of confidence in the team's ability to achieve their goals and objectives. Please explain.
- Rate on a scale of 1 (none or low) to 5 (high) your level of motivation to achieve the team's goals and objectives. Please explain.
- Rate on a scale of 1 (none or low) to 5 (high) your ability to focus on the team's goals and objectives in team meetings. Please explain.
- Rate on a scale of 1 (none or low) to 5 (high) the level of knowledge diversity relevant to the team's goals and objectives that team members bring. Please explain.

The simple team creativity assessment uses the same ranking scale as the team climate health check (1 means none or low, 2 means lower than average, 3 means average, 4 means higher than average, and 5 means high). The team leader can process the rankings and comments either inside or outside of the team meeting. The collated responses and comments are discussed in a meeting to develop action items and next steps to address the lowest-scoring statements taking into account the comments. You might consider the following aspects for ways to improve each dimension.

Ways to improve confidence in achieving team goals and objectives:

- Increase the autonomy of team members in pursuing team goals and objectives when articulating action items.
- Do group exercises related to team goals and objectives that enable team members to get to know one another better.
- Try an improv exercise to improve the listening skills of team members.[14]

Ways to improve team goal motivation:
- Point out the benefits of achieving a team goal and the concerns that will be addressed or limitations that will be removed in achieving that goal.
- View setbacks and failures in team goal pursuit as opportunities to learn and as a new problem for the team to display their creativity and innovation.
- Develop a communication plan for inside and outside of team meetings.

Ways to improve focus:
- Do a group exercise to clarify the results and deliverables for the team.
- Do a group exercise to articulate a problem statement (a statement that begins with "How might," "How to," or "In what ways might") that catalyzes the type of creativity needed.

Ways to improve access to knowledge diversity:
- Take a break for each team member to consider and document their perspective on the problem at hand; then have the team leader read each perspective for consideration.
- Go around the room to have each team member contribute to a given discussion or decision.
- Do a thinking-talents exercise[15] and plot the results for the team on a problem-solving styles matrix.

The simple creativity assessment is a starting point for a team to develop a climate conducive to creativity. The next section considers the challenges of creativity for team members and teams in a little more depth.

THE CHALLENGES OF TEAM CREATIVITY

People who study creativity in different contexts have produced different definitions of creativity that share fundamental elements. Creativity is not context dependent and can show up in many different forms inside and outside organizations. It can show up in a poem, movie, drawing, Super Bowl half-time performance, soccer goal, business proposal, business process, or new product or service offering. The two fundamental elements that characterize creativity are newness and helpfulness.

Team creativity happens when team members find new associations that are useful to the team's work. Our nonconscious brain is wired to find patterns but not the new associations needed for creativity. Creativity does not come naturally from our nonconscious brain because creativity takes engaging the limited capacity of our conscious-thinking brain.[16] Creativity is challenging because we are working against our brain's natural wiring to find patterns. Creativity is also challenging because it is misunderstood. Widespread creativity myths can be a barrier to creativity. We'll bust three creativity myths here.

First is the "born with it" creativity myth, which says that you are creative because you are born with the ability to be creative. Researchers have found that when people are engaged in creative tasks, they are using the same brain regions that are used for noncreative tasks.[17] If the same brain regions are used for noncreative and creative tasks, then we all have the basic brain hardware needed to be creative. But hardware doesn't work well without the right software. So people need to develop the software required for creativity, which is the process of using the brain hardware to get the desired result. Process is something that can be taught and learned. In fact, creativity guru Dr. Keith Sawyer describes how to improve creativity using the eight components of ask, look, learn, play, think, fuse, choose, and make.[18] You can become more creative if you believe that creativity can be improved and you seek to learn how to improve creativity. You can't become more creative if you believe that creativity is a fixed trait—something you are born with or not born with. The "born with it" creativity myth is busted!

Second is the "lone inventor" creativity myth, which says that the best ideas come from one person working alone. In fact, researchers have found that traditional brainstorming does not produce the best ideas.[19] However, researchers have also found that a mixture of working alone and working with others in a supportive climate for creativity leads to the best ideas. Further, solitary creative acts are made more creative from the input of others. For example, J. R. R. Tolkien, author of the acclaimed *Lord of the Rings* trilogy and *The Hobbit*, worked with C. S. Lewis and others in a group called The Inklings to improve on writing mythical fiction. Tolkien credited The Inklings for the production of his literary masterpieces. The "lone inventor" creativity myth is busted!

Third is the "eureka" creativity myth, which stipulates that creativity is born from an "aha" moment out of nowhere. There is such a thing as an insight that feels like an "aha" moment, and insights are a very important part of creativity. But an insight doesn't come out of nowhere. A prerequisite for an insight is getting stuck on a problem. That is, you first need to be working on a problem and then get stuck as the first step to having an insight.[20] The second step to having an insight is taking your focus away from the problem and getting in a more relaxed state of attention. For example, exercising, daydreaming, walking, napping, taking a coffee break, taking a shower, and meditating are different ways to get into a relaxed state of attention. The third step is generating inward focus by tampering down stimulation of the visual cortex by what you're seeing around you. Inward focus enhances your ability to listen for and be aware of the weak nonconscious associations that your brain is trying to make relative to the problem. Finally, insight happens when a new and useful connection is made to help get you unstuck on the problem. Marc Benioff, CEO and founder of multibillion dollar sales giant Salesforce, has created "mindfulness zones" for employees on every floor because he practices meditation to spur creativity and innovation.[21] The "eureka" creativity myth has been busted!

Team leaders and team members need to bust creativity myths for themselves and for their teams because creativity is the raw material for problem solving and opportunity identification. Teams have been found to be more likely than individuals to develop innovative solutions, which is one of the reasons that much of the work we do happens in teams.[22] Yet creativity can be expressed and flourish in a team only when the climate makes all members comfortable. For example, members need to feel psychological safety in a group to be able to express their creative ideas and thoughts.[23] One of two key elements of psychological safety in a team is members expressing humility toward the problem or opportunity requiring creativity. Humility takes sharing what you know to help with the problem or opportunity and being open to the things you don't know that may help with the problem or opportunity. The second of two key elements of psychological safety in a team is member curiosity to learn from others to help with the problem or opportunity. Situational humility and curiosity toward others together fuel the trust needed between members to support creativity. Curiosity toward others helps minimize interpersonal conflict, which can be a barrier to creativity. Curiosity toward others also helps increase risk taking, which improves creativity in a group. Situational humility helps group members offer and discuss the merit of ideas, which increases group creativity. Situational humility also helps group members enjoy the creative process and stay engaged in the face of difficulty, which both increase group creativity.

Team leaders and team members have similar roles to play in establishing a good team climate to promote creativity. But the roles of leaders and members in establishing an overall good climate for team performance differ in some ways. Power and competition are two dynamics that impact team climate and are associated more with team leadership than with members.

LEADERSHIP DYNAMICS IMPACTING TEAM CLIMATE

Two leadership dynamics are important to the team climate needed for high performance. One is the use of power within the team. A second is the use of competition to drive performance. Both power and competition can be powerful motivators for behaviors that drive results and, conversely, they can drive behaviors that limit performance.

Power is an inescapable element of team climate: it is the ability to influence the behavior of other people. A team without power accomplishes nothing because a team consisting of members who can't influence each other will spin its wheels. I was on a community team in which each member, including the team leader, did not know how to influence each other. One person would say, "I think we should . . .," the next person would say, "I don't know about that, but I think we should . . .," and so on around the room until we had ten different proposals on the table with no discussion, no decision, and no next steps. A team with the wrong kinds of power also accomplishes nothing. I was on a work team in which the team leader dictated in great detail what was going to be done, but because no one was motivated to take instruction from a dictator, nothing happened between meetings. A team with the right kinds of power, however, is unstoppable.

Research shows that some forms of power decrease the performance and discretionary effort by others.[24] Specifically, the use of coercive, reward, or positional power by a team leader decreases the efforts of team members. With coercive power a person acts on another's behalf because of a credible threat, such as a boss warning a subordinate of a demotion if they do not meet a specific performance goal. The use of coercive power on teams can be more subtle, such as a more experienced employee blaming a less experienced employee for a work problem when the less experienced employee is not in the room. Reward power is the use of compliments, personal development incentives, career visibility incentives, and salary incentives to influence the behavior of another member. I had a boss compliment me on my initiative and creativity in taking over a project he didn't have time to manage, and I worked even harder on the project without additional benefit to me. Finally, positional power is using formal authority in the organization's hierarchy to get people to behave in a certain way. An example of positional power is a team leader who asks a member who also happens to be the leader's subordinate to complete an action item that no one else on the team volunteers to take on.

Research shows that the use of expert power or referent power increases the performance and discretionary efforts of others. Expert power is the extent to which your expertise drives others to want to work with you. If you bring a loved one to the emergency room, then you are going to listen to the medical professional with ten years of experience over the second-year medical student on rotations. Referent power is the extent to which respect drives others to want to work with you. For example, my boss's superior called me into his office to ask me if everything was alright with my boss because my boss had criticized my team leadership skills in a recent staff meeting with the superior. My boss's superior did the honorable thing of providing examples of me excelling in team leadership roles to squash the criticism in the meeting—that is behavior worthy of respect. The more expert power and referent power used in a team, the higher the performance of that team.

Competence is an important ingredient for developing expert power. Expert power is more important than the positional power that comes from holding the title of team leader for promoting performance by team members. When a leader lacks the subject matter expertise for a particular team, one tactic is to recruit an assistant with an interest in developing the subject matter expertise. The content support needed by the leader can be positioned to the assistant as a career development opportunity. The leader would retain the title, and the recruited assistant would become the facilitator and subject matter expert for the team. The assistant would need to devote time for developing expertise in the subject matter area and for supporting the leader's learning needs. I served the role of facilitator and subject matter expert for a Sustainability Community Council for a company's material science business. The council was created and led by the chief operations officer who did not have time to develop the needed subject matter expertise to support the council's charter. Serving this role was an add-on to my full-time job responsibilities and was a lot of additional work, but the work led to a promotion for me two years later to head of sustainability for the company's businesses reporting to the CEO for North America.

A second tactic for a team leader to develop needed competence and expert power is to recruit an external subject matter expert. For example, I established a retainer for a corporate sustainability guru when I was developing the sustainability strategy with a Corporate Sustainability Community Council. I also served as an external subject matter expert for a company that was developing an idea management system when I was working as an independent consultant. Hiring an external consultant is a fast and efficient way for a team leader to gain needed expertise as long as there is budget to use this tactic.

Character is an important ingredient for developing referent power. Referent power, like expert power, is more important than the positional power that comes from holding the title of team leader in eliciting performance from team members. Referent power comes from people skills. A leader can work with a leadership development coach for guidance on how to develop referent power with members and enable them to perform at a high level.

The competence needed for expert power and the character needed for referent power are two core ingredients for building trust with others.[25] Building trust between the team leader and team members correlates with team performance. A final tactic for improving the use of expert and referent power in a team is for members, including the leader, to do a self-assessment of team performance. The team performance self-assessment shared here is a modified version of an in-house assessment used to improve the performance of a strategy team that I led in a corporate environment. This assessment is a great tool when the leader has a thick skin and when the leader will follow up on the assessment results to improve team performance.

TEAM PERFORMANCE SELF-ASSESSMENT

1. The team leader introduces the team performance self-assessment as an opportunity to improve team results and asks for team members to commit to doing the assessment.
2. The team leader explains that each statement on the assessment is to be ranked on a scale from 1 for strongly

disagree to 5 for strongly agree (2 is disagree somewhat, 3 is neither disagree nor agree, 4 is agree somewhat). The leader encourages team members to provide comments to help explain answers. Members are instructed to email their responses to a person outside the team who will collate the responses for anonymity.

3. The following twenty-seven statements (seventeen are team character assessment statements, and ten are team competence assessment statements) are provided to team members for ranking on a scale of 1 to 5:

Team Character Assessment Statements

- Overall, I trust (defined as fairness, respect, and credibility) my team members.
- Members of my team consistently demonstrate respect for the individual.
- On my team, employees are treated equally and fairly with regard to rewards, recognition, and opportunities.
- My team solicits and actively considers my opinion when making decisions that affect me.
- Team members keep the commitments and promises they make to each other.
- My team respects the confidentiality of information provided by our external stakeholders (the people most impacted by our work) and by other people outside the team.
- I am encouraged by my team to express my opinions in an open and truthful manner without fear of repercussion.
- Members of my team generally agree on the right way and wrong way to do things.
- When there is a problem that needs to be solved, my teammates often ask for my input and suggestions.

- My team is tolerant of failure when a teammate takes initiative to improve products, processes, or services.
- Generally, team members work together rather than compete with each other.
- My team recognizes and appreciates teammates' suggestions for new ideas or improvements.
- My team actively supports teammates' efforts to advance and to enhance their skills and/or education.
- Members of my team motivate each other to go above and beyond.
- New ideas and improvements that I suggest are always considered by my team.
- My team keeps confidential information to ourselves (for example, information stipulated as confidential by law and/or by policy).
- My answers to this survey will be considered and will make a difference.

Team Competence Assessment Statements

- The information my team needs to perform our job effectively is readily shared.
- My team normally explores alternatives before making major changes.
- Doing a good job is usually recognized by my team and team leader.
- My team complies with the laws, regulations, and good business practices that relate to our work.
- My team holds team members accountable for getting their jobs done.
- My team understands their role in accomplishing goals and objectives.

- Excellence in both what we deliver and how we deliver it is highly valued by my team.
- My team is dedicated to delivering value as defined by our stakeholders (the people most impacted by our work).
- My team consistently meets or exceeds our internal and/or external customer expectations.
- My team prioritizes, makes decisions, and acts quickly.

4. The collated responses are discussed by the team. Areas for improvement are identified, and action items to realize improvement are formulated, prioritized, and monitored for completion.

Just like some forms of power are conducive to effort while other forms of power are not, some forms of competition lead to improved performance and other forms of competition do not. Certain forms of competition can breed high engagement and excellence. For example, my husband and I decided to enter a workplace photo competition—back when there were no cell phones, let alone cameras in cell phones. My husband taunted me with his superior Pentax camera and expensive attachments compared to my tawdry automatic Olympus camera. However, what I lacked in equipment, I made up for in artistic abilities. The result was that I won second place overall in the competition, which gave me a plaque and a large framed version of my winning photograph, while my husband got an "honorable mention" ribbon. Regardless, we were both highly engaged in the competition, and I can say that the competition brought out my best performance in photography.

While competition can increase engagement and performance, it can also be a barrier to them. I remember when another PhD chemical engineer and I were new to a polymer research group, both of us full of ambition. The research group made high-performance composites for car interiors. The other engineer had an overt competitive attitude of "may the best PhD win." Initially, I tried working with this other engineer, but I quickly started avoiding him because my ability to collaborate and create suffered when I tried to work with him. Instead, I collaborated with other seasoned engineers in the group, and my creativity blossomed. While the new engineer and I did some good work on our own, I believe we could have done even better work together. In this case, competition led to mistrust, disengagement, and a lost opportunity for improved performance.

It turns out that mindset is the key to determining whether competition will lead to engagement and increased performance by a team. Researchers have found a relationship between mindset toward achieving a goal and performance toward that goal.[26] Specifically, if your mindset in competing toward a goal is to avoid looking bad compared to others, then your performance will suffer. In my case with the PhD work colleague, I did not want him to make me look bad in front of our coworkers because I was new to the group, and I wanted to make a good impression. I was concerned with looking bad because I didn't have as much confidence in my abilities as this other engineer had in his abilities. My mindset to avoid looking bad in interacting with this other engineer decreased my performance in trying to work with him.

On the other hand, if your mindset in competing toward a goal is to look good compared to others, then your performance will be enhanced because you will work harder. In the workplace photo competition with my husband, I wanted to showcase my artistic ability to make me look good compared to others. My second-place finish in the photo contest was thanks to my mindset to look good and also afforded me spousal bragging rights.

Expectation is another concern when using competition to improve performance. If you have too high or too low of an expectation for performance against a goal, whether or not the expectation is reasonable, then you can end up a sore loser or a sore winner. The behaviors of sore losers and sore winners are annoying everywhere but especially in workplaces. Deriding my boss for placing lower in a fund-raising competition would not help my chances to be recommended for the next promotion.

Researchers have discovered a relationship between expected performance against a goal and our critical thinking ability.[27] Critical thinking, which includes situation assessment, problem solving, strategic thinking, decision-making, idea generation, and innovation, is key to team goals in the workplace. But too little expectation or too much expectation degrades our ability for critical thinking because emotional thinking is triggered in the nonconscious brain as a distraction. For example, too little expectation for performance against a goal can cause indifference or fear toward goal pursuit. Conversely, too much expectation about our ability to perform against a goal can cause doubt and worry when our performance shows signs of diverting away from the expectation. Finally, we can experience strong negative emotion when there is a big difference between what we expect to happen and what actually happens. The bigger the expectation, the bigger the anticipated reward, and the bigger the disappointment when the reward does not materialize. I remember watching an AFC Championship game between the Jacksonville Jaguars and the New England Patriots and being elated at half-time because the Jaguars were winning and I expected the Patriots to lose. Not even my husband could pick up the pieces when the Jaguars lost the game because I was so mad and such a sore loser as a result. Of course, it didn't help that my youngest brother, a Patriots fan, called me to exhibit the sore winner behavior of gloating about the win!

There are both benefits and trappings to using competition to improve performance. Competition is a great strategy to improve performance when the benefits can be leveraged and the trappings avoided. The potential benefits include an opportunity to look good compared to others, improved skills and abilities, and good behavior whether you win or lose. The potential trappings include a risk of looking bad compared to others, a lost opportunity for learning and personal growth, and bad behavior relative to the competition outcome.

Team leaders can use three tactics to harvest the benefits and avoid the trappings of competition. First, the leader can help those competing find a connection between the goal and their sources of intrinsic motivation.[28] Motivation to pursue a goal is increased when we see a connection between why a goal is important to pursue and something we care about. Second, the leader can help those competing to focus more on how to accomplish the goal rather than on who is going to win or lose. Specifically, the leader wants to help those competing focus on the unique skills and talents they can showcase in pursuit of the goal. And third, the leader can cultivate a growth mindset toward the competition by framing the goal pursuit as an opportunity for participants to learn and develop. The opposite of a growth mindset is a fixed mindset. The leader can avoid triggering a fixed mindset by recognizing the contribution of effort and hard work by those competing and not comparing traits like intelligence or creativity of the competitors. Now we turn to the role that team members play in establishing a team climate that promotes team performance.

TEAM MEMBER ROLE IN TEAM CLIMATE

A team member's ability to contribute to a team depends on their level of comfort contributing in team meetings. If a member does not feel comfortable contributing during a meeting, then that person is not going to contribute at all or is not going to contribute in helpful ways. If all members are not contributing, then the team is falling short of their performance potential. Therefore, a member needs to notice when a change in their comfort level to contribute has occurred during a meeting and needs to take action to rectify the situation.

The action a team member needs to take when they become uncomfortable contributing to a team meeting depends on the type of discomfort they are experiencing. For example, if that person is experiencing fear or anger, then they need to first dissipate the negative emotion. I remember being in a staff meeting with a new boss who told me, in front of my colleagues, that he did not understand the value my group produced for the organization. My face flushed red, and I wanted to go on the attack to protect myself and my group. When you experience strong negative emotion, you act out or withdraw as needed to protect yourself without thinking about it. But in a team meeting, you want to contribute your thinking. A technique to dissipate strong negative emotion is to take three to five deep and slow breaths in and out until you can think clearly again. Fortunately, I was familiar with this breathing technique and used it to dissipate my anger so I could offer a helpful suggestion. In this case, I asked for a one-on-one meeting to brainstorm ways to better demonstrate my group's value to the organization.

A team member may experience milder negative emotions like annoyance or frustration to prevent them from contributing in a team meeting. Again, the negative emotion needs to be dissipated before that person can contribute their critical thinking to the meeting. In the case of milder negative emotions, the member needs to check that there is solid evidence for the basis of their negative emotion. For example, someone saying, "It's none of your business" can be taken personally when what they really meant was, "You are intruding on something I consider to be part of my job responsibility." It is prudent for a member to ask questions to check their interpretation of what was said before saying something they may regret later. For example, a member can ask, "What do you mean?" or "How is this topic troubling you?" or "In what ways is the discussion problematic?" Questioning will help the member reinterpret what was said to dissipate the negative emotion they are feeling. Questioning to explore if there is a good reason to feel negative emotion will help uncover the issue that really needs to be discussed and get members back on track contributing to the team.

Finally, a team member may experience confusion to prevent them from contributing in a team meeting. They cannot let confusion get in the way of contribution because confusion is an opportunity for learning and increased performance. A member who experiences confusion can say, "I'm not clear on what we have been asked to do" or "I'm not clear on how what we are discussing relates to our team goal" and so on. If that person is experiencing confusion about a problem that the team has been asked to address, then they can try four tactics to improve the situation.

The first tactic to clarify a problem that the team leader has raised is to test the worthiness of the problem. Generating ideas and solutions is time consuming in a meeting and should be reserved for the most worthwhile problems. The team member can ask: "What direction is this problem directing effort?" Next, they can ask: "Why is this direction worthwhile?" The answers to these questions will clarify the effort needed by members and help direct their effort in the most worthwhile direction.

A second tactic is to test the helpfulness of the problem to the team's goals. A team member can suggest that the team come up with new questions that the problem leads to and consider the helpfulness of those new questions to the team's goals. The member can explain that the more new questions a problem statement generates, the better the ideas and solutions that can be developed to address the problem. The team then can refine the problem as needed to trigger better or more added questions before brainstorming ideas and solutions.

A third tactic is to use the ladder of abstraction, which is a technique to factor in the team's sphere of influence in tackling a problem. A team member can suggest using this technique to fine-tune a problem for maximum impact. The first step is to ask "how" for the problem to get more concrete versions of the problem. Keep asking "how" to get as many new versions of the problem as possible that are more concrete versions and write all the new versions of the problem down for all to see. Next, ask "why" for the original problem to get more abstract versions of the problem. Keep asking "why" to get as many new versions of the problem as possible that are more abstract versions and write all these new versions of the problem down for all to see. Finally, revise the original problem statement based on the new problem statements to maximize possible impact by the team and ensure that addressing the problem is within the team's ability to influence.

A final tactic a team member can try to clarify a problem that the team leader has raised is to test whether the types of ideas and solutions triggered by the problem are the kinds of things that the team needs. For example, the member can consider whether the problem is worded to catalyze higher levels of novelty than the "as is" situation. They can also consider how hard it is to generate ideas and solutions for the problem. The harder it is to generate ideas and solutions, the fewer ideas and solutions will be generated and the less likely an attractive idea or solution will be found. The problem can be refined to address the issues encountered in testing brainstorming for the problem.

Team climate is something that the team leader and team members can control but is often overlooked as an important ingredient to a team's performance. Team climate problems are tricky to resolve because the symptoms don't point to the solution needed. Rather, a team needs an assessment technique to uncover solutions to team climate problems. In the interim, leaders need to be aware of the negative impacts that power and competition can have on team climate, and members need to address their sources of discomfort in team meetings. The next chapter focuses on team operation, which is a specific aspect of team climate.

Here are some reflection exercises and questions for this chapter on team climate to enhance learning:

- Recall a team that you enjoyed participating in. In what ways did the team leader and other team members make your team experience enjoyable?
- What about promoting creativity discussed in this chapter surprised you?
- In what ways might you improve your creativity?

CHAPTER 6

Troubleshooting
Team Operation

I was in another dull department meeting with one presenter after another telling me things I needed to know about safety, compliance, and the business. Department meetings were monthly and mandatory for noncritical workers like me. I went to these meetings because they served donuts and Danishes and because I was worried my boss would notice if I wasn't there. But this department meeting changed for the better when the third speaker carried in a metal stand holding a large pad. He started his presentation by asking a question and calling on audience members for answers. He jotted down the answers on the large pad attached to the metal stand using a Sharpie marker, and he organized the input as he went to make his first point. After making his point, he ripped the page where he had been writing off the pad and moved on to a different question to make his next point. I was mesmerized by how much the speaker and the audience enjoyed the interaction. I could feel energy and positive emotion permeate the room that did not exist before this third speaker. The speaker with the flipchart was able to impact the people in the room like no other presenter by operating in a different way.

Workplace professionals are hired for their expertise. When asked to give a presentation at a meeting, they will focus on what they know because they were hired for that reason. However, presenters focused on content have limited impact on meeting participants. Participants must invest time and intellect to understand a presentation, so they expect a return just like you expect a job from the money and time you invest to earn a college degree. Participants need to understand why a presentation is valuable to them and how that value will be unlocked before investing their time and intellect. Too often, work teams focus on content but not on the "why" and "how" members should engage. Teams increase the quality of member participation and meeting outcomes when the "why" and "how" of meeting topics are addressed in meeting operation.

In 1996 Bill Gates declared that content is king on the Internet, but that doesn't mean content is king on teams. In fact, viewing content as king is a problem for team performance. A focus on content limits what is possible for a team because it's often what you don't know you know or what you don't know you don't know that unleashes high performance and opportunities. I know that too much focus on content is a problem for team performance because of the feedback I get from team members following my meetings. Here is one example of what a member told me worked well for them in my meeting: "Brainstorming in the morning was very energetic and productive. Format in general was organized well and kept discussion moving forward." This member talks about the "how" (brainstorming and format) of the meeting as what worked well for them. Another example: "It was really terrific. Well organized, goal was clear, people were engaged. I was skeptical at beginning that the time would be worthwhile, but I'm now well convinced it was worth it. I also liked how well integrated each part was (i.e., take sticky notes made in one exercise and use it in the next exercise)." This member was skeptical entering the meeting based on content alone, but the "why" ("goal was clear") and the "how" (organization and integration) of the meeting changed their mind.

Team operation is what determines if the "why" and "how" of meeting topics are addressed. It is the way the team leader and team members act in a meeting. Chemical engineers and mathematicians understand an operation to be a series of steps to convert inputs into outputs. Similarly, operation in a team meeting is the sequence of steps to convert the meeting inputs into the meeting outputs. Meeting inputs include the members, the logistics, office tools, prework, and information supplied at the meeting, and meeting outputs are the outcomes. But converting inputs to outputs, like lots of social endeavors, is harder than it sounds because it is fraught with things that can go wrong.

TYPES OF TEAM OPERATION PROBLEMS

A team has operation problems when there is a lack of fundamental facilitation practices. Such practices are techniques that focus on creating an environment of engagement for participants. Creating the right environment for engagement may sound more like leadership than facilitation. But facilitating a team meeting is not the same thing as leading one. A facilitator leads the process for a meeting but does not engage in the content of the meeting other than to guide the type of content expected as a meeting outcome. A leader holds the vision for the team and is enough of a content expert to understand the steps needed to move toward the vision and to exercise expert power. A leader may act as a facilitator but only when it is appropriate to not contribute content and only if they have the skill set needed to be a good facilitator. You can evaluate your facilitator skill set and learn how to improve facilitation skills by using Fulcrum's Facilitation Assessment (to get a free copy of the assessment, email "facilitation free at last" in the title to *valerie. patrick@fulcrumconnection.com*).

Some of the skills needed by facilitators are developed from leadership experiences. For example, facilitators need to be comfortable standing up before a group of people and guiding them to a destination. Facilitators also need to be good public speakers who exude positive energy, enthusiasm, and confidence when speaking to be able to engage meeting participants. Effective interpersonal skills help facilitators address dysfunctional behavior in a way that keeps participants engaged and contributing to the meeting outcomes. Finally, facilitators need to commit to and deliver the meeting outcomes they agreed to target with the team leader.

The relationship between facilitation and leadership is like the relationship between innovation and creativity. Specifically, you can't have innovation without creativity, but not all creativity leads to innovation. Similarly, you can't facilitate without leadership, but not all leadership produces facilitation. Facilitation and innovation focus on implementation to create value while leadership and creativity are skills to enable facilitation and innovation. For example, innovators implement ideas that come from creativity, and facilitators produce meeting outcomes specified by a team leader. Facilitation provides the structure and focus needed for a group of people to work together toward specified outcomes while leadership specifies the outcomes. Chapter 3 focused on the tactics needed to address team leadership problems, and this chapter focuses on the fundamental facilitation tactics needed to troubleshoot team operation problems.

One of four types of team operation problems is poor planning. Poor planning for a team meeting can show up in different ways. For example, it can result in no meeting agenda or in an agenda supplied to team members too late for them to do meaningful preparation for the meeting. Another way that poor planning shows up in a meeting is a team falling behind on an agenda with no plan for how to address the situation. Poor planning is also the culprit when members are confused about how to do an assigned meeting task or how to provide requested input. Finally, it causes members to question why they are working on a meeting task and to be confused about meeting outcomes.

A second type of team operation problem is unequal participation by team members. An important goal of a facilitator is equal participation across members because the more equal the participation, the higher the team performance.[1] In fact, the International Association of Facilitators outlines eighteen core competencies for facilitator certification, and more than half (61 percent) address equal participation across members.[2] Unequal participation can appear as one member dominating the meeting or no response to a team leader's request for input.

A third type of team operation problem is consensus issues. Consensus in a group is agreement based on a specified consensus process. There is a spectrum of consensus processes from one person making the decision on one end, to majority rules in the middle, to 100 percent agreement on the other end. One example of a consensus issue is team members complaining about team decisions outside of team meetings. A member disagrees with a team's decision outside the meeting because they did not understand the group consensus process, or they felt the group consensus process was the wrong one. Another example is persistent disagreement about important content like a team goal, an action point, or the people most impacted by the team's work. Persistent disagreement is an indication that a group consensus process has been miscommunicated or is missing but needed.

A fourth type of team operation problem is an implementation challenge. For example, the team does not have clear deliverables with time frames, or the team is not meeting their deliverables on time. Another indication of an implementation challenge is team members not completing action items between meetings. Finally, members express disappointment with the team's accomplishments or with meeting-to-meeting progress when there are implementation shortcomings.

This chapter starts with a discussion of team operation basics, which focus on processes for planning meetings and increased participation across team members. Next, tactics are provided for team operation basics specific to proper planning and member participation. There is also a deep dive into the science of and methods for engagement. Finally, the chapter discusses operation tactics to improve consensus and implementation.

TEAM OPERATION 101

Basic processes for team operation can be remembered as the *ABC'S* of team operation. ABC'S is an acronym that stands for Agendas, Barters, Charters, and Starters/Enders. The use of the ABC'S for team operation focuses on improving planning and participation for more success and effectiveness in team meetings.

Developing a charter is an important process for a team that will be together for a year or longer. A charter provides the scope of work for team members, such as the team's purpose, resources, boundaries, barriers, deliverables, and endpoint. As such, a charter provides certainty about a team's goal to help focus member effort toward that goal. A charter helps eliminate the natural negative bias toward teams that can occur when members doubt the ability of the team to do constructive and worthwhile work. Charters can also be used to provide guidance and context for team meeting agendas. A sample team charter is provided here, but there are many different formats for team charters to explore and customize to a given team's needs and preferences.

SAMPLE TEAM CHARTER

Team Name: Corporate Sustainability Community Council

Purpose and Scope:

[Company Name] has great potential to reap reward from the sustainability movement by being part of the solution to some of the most pressing environmental challenges. [Company Name] also faces risks from the sustainability movement that need to be managed to mitigate adverse impact on our businesses. Finally, the best ideas to reap reward and mitigate risk can come from a number of different sources as is the known experience with innovation.

The topic of sustainability is both intellectually challenging and critically important. It is highly unlikely for empowered individuals to "get it right" or engage the topic in the most value-producing way both from an intellectual standpoint and a resource standpoint. This Community Council provides a mechanism to collect and vet scattered knowledge and activity, bring in external experts to fill knowledge gaps as needed, incorporate broad stakeholder input, and leverage the resulting knowledge and insights to pursue sustainable development on a vetted path forward that delivers value to the company.

Team Mission:

Coordinate, guide, and catalyze the incorporation of sustainability into business strategy and daily operations in a way that preserves/enhances [Company Name]'s reputation while mitigating risk or creating reward via cost savings or increased revenue.

Team Vision: Be a recognized sustainable development leader in North America.

Team Leader: [Name and Title]

Team Sponsor: [Name and Title]

Team Members: [List of Names and Titles]

Boundaries and Barriers:

The stakeholders to our team's sustainability efforts include the Regional Council, employees, customers, relevant governmental agencies and representatives, relevant NGOs, investors, stockholders, and the communities in which we work.

The information resources for this team include raw material suppliers to all [Company Name] operations, [Company Name] personnel involved in current and future sustainability activities, universities and colleges that can support our sustainability activities and strategy, open innovation partners that support our sustainability activities and strategy, consultants that support our sustainability activities and strategy, and other external resources that fill our knowledge gaps with respect to sustainability.

The kinds of team decisions that need approval are those that require corporate spending. The kinds of team decisions that don't need approval are those that can be handled within the business or function represented and those supporting the execution of sponsor-supported deliverables.

We will implement actions that the Council supports and that fulfill our mission and vision.

Deliverables:

1. Pursue, on an ongoing basis, contextual intelligence across [Company Name] in sustainability.
2. Achieve and maintain sustainability thought leadership for [Company Name].
3. Develop and maintain a process to track progress against our vision to be a recognized sustainable development leader in North America.
4. Determine and execute next steps from the results of the company-wide sustainability forum held with external stakeholders.
5. Define what a project candidate for sustainability looks like.
6. Build and maintain a portfolio of sustainability projects.
7. Formulate and feed sustainability insights into business strategy and day-to-day operations for creation and implementation of projects that preserve/enhance [Company Name]'s reputation while mitigating risk, creating cost savings, or increasing revenues.

First Year Goals:

1. Define process to pursue contextual intelligence in sustainability across [Company Name] by the end of the first quarter of this year.
2. Determine method to achieve and maintain sustainability thought leadership by the end of the second quarter of this year.
3. Develop and maintain a process to track progress against our vision by the end of the third quarter of this year.
4. Determine and execute next steps from the company-wide sustainability forum by February of this year.
5. Define what a project candidate for sustainability looks like by April of this year.
6. Propose sustainability projects to pursue by year-end.
7. Determine a mechanism to formulate and feed sustainability insights into business strategy and day-to-day operations on an ongoing basis by year-end.

Resources, Tools, and Budget:

The Team will identify needed resources to implement the tactical plans. The Sponsor will be our liaison to work with functions, sites, and colleagues as needed to ask for funding and resources to support our work. Any Corporate funding needs will need a business proposal and approval.

Agendas, barters, starters, and enders are processes that benefit every team meeting for effective team operation. An agenda is a process guide that informs team members of the content, process, and logistics for a meeting. A team leader who provides a high-quality agenda to members well ahead of a meeting is signaling that they want members prepared to provide good input at the meeting. In contrast, a great way for a leader to keep total control of a meeting is to not provide an agenda before a meeting or not provide an agenda at all. Barters are a simple process to boost efficiency and effectiveness during a meeting based on the social need for fairness. A barter is an exchange of individual work by members for something beneficial to the team. Starters and enders are processes used at the beginning and end of meetings to build social connection beyond that from meeting together. Starters are also known as ice-breakers or warm-ups, and enders are also known as meeting evaluations. Specific examples of agendas, barters, starters, and enders are provided later in this chapter. The rest of this section focuses on proven steps for proper planning of meetings.

I have worked as a Certified Professional Facilitator for the last six years and have learned that proper planning surpasses all else in team operation. In fact, the work a facilitator does before a team meeting has a larger contribution to meeting success than the work they do during the meeting. For example, a plan enables a facilitator to discern when to go off-plan and how to go off-plan with intention and still achieve the desired meeting outcomes.[3] The three most important components to meeting planning are the meeting purpose, objectives, and outcomes. The purpose communicates the "why" to have the meeting to members. The objectives prioritize the scope of what is possible given who will be participating in the team meeting and the time available for the meeting. The outcomes are the desired product of the meeting.[4,5]

A powerful meeting purpose articulates the path for a team to get from where they are to a desired future state. A sample meeting purpose is as follows: Build consensus across key stakeholders for design principles of a first idea management system to start implementation. In this case, the current state is no idea management system. The desired future state is to implement an idea management system that meets the needs of key stakeholders. The path is to build consensus for principles to design an idea management system so that the system can be selected and implemented.

The meeting objectives are the steps needed for team members to achieve the meeting purpose in the time allotted. Planning fallacy is a concern in developing meeting objectives because it is the natural tendency to believe you can get more done in the time allotted than you actually can get done. Meeting objectives are developed by thinking about the sequence of activities needed before, during, and after the meeting to achieve the meeting purpose. Sample meeting objectives for the purpose of building consensus across key stakeholders for design principles are as follows:

- Share findings from primary research (interviews) and secondary research on idea management.
- Involve key stakeholders in shaping the organization's approach to idea management.
- Empower the implementation team with next steps to implement idea management at our organization.

The first objective addresses what needs to happen before the meeting to establish the content needed for the meeting purpose. The second addresses what needs to happen during the meeting to achieve the purpose. The third addresses what achieving the purpose can enable after the meeting. Let's zoom in on these objectives to help shape the outcomes for the meeting.

The first meeting objective indicates the type of preparation needed for the meeting. In this case, part of the meeting preparation is interviewing a representative sample of key stakeholders to understand their thoughts and knowledge about idea management. Another part of the preparation is comparing the input collected from the interviews to best practices gleaned from secondary research on idea management. The first objective provides a content basis for discussion and decisions by a group of people toward the purpose. The second and third objectives provide insight into how the preparation can best be used toward the purpose in the time allotted for the meeting. In this case, the prework will be used to draft a set of guiding and design principles on idea management for team members to react to and provide input for in the meeting.

Thus, the second objective is accomplished by additional prework so that input on draft guiding and design principles can be solicited during the meeting. If members can feel confident they are providing input on thoroughly vetted content, then they are more likely to support follow-up actions needed to support the third objective.

The outcomes for the meeting are the deliverables. The outcomes put focus on the type of activities that will be incorporated into the meeting. For the preceding meeting purpose and objectives, sample meeting outcomes are as follows:

- Consensus from participants on guiding principles for idea management at our company
- Consensus from participants on design principles for idea management at our company
- Support from participants for the implementation team to start their work

This example illustrates that developing a meeting purpose, objectives, and outcomes is a creative and nonlinear process that takes critical thinking. For example, the meeting purpose to build consensus across stakeholders for an idea management system could be pursued by identifying and then voting on different systems available. Further, the objective to share findings from primary and secondary research appears to have nothing to do with consensus. But the stakeholders are scientists who will be reluctant to support a course of action unless there is evidence to back it up, so a decision would tend to get bogged down with critical debate. Also, the meeting is scheduled for a half day, which would not be enough time to demonstrate different systems available, answer questions, take a vote, and then have the discussion needed to reach consensus. So planning needs to take into account how to be successful in achieving purpose given the anticipated behavior of participants and the time allotted. Taking into account participant behavior and the time allotted can be challenging and requires some creativity and skill to address the challenges identified.

Even though meeting planning is a nonlinear process, the heart of team operation is a linear, step-by-step process that is easy for participants to follow and designed to achieve outcomes in the allotted time. In this case, team members need a way to consider the merits and limitations of both the draft guiding and design principles and to address the top limitations identified. Identifying and addressing the limitations of the draft principles will pave the way for consensus and support of next steps. Keep in mind that team operation can also include prework for meeting participants like sending the draft principles ahead of time for consideration. The intricacies of meeting planning and process are discussed in chapter 7 on meeting design.

In addition to meeting planning and process, successful team operation takes a number of tactics to support the process. These operational tactics include a meeting agenda, office tools needed to support the meeting activities outlined in the agenda, content needed to support the team activities, a way to capture team member input, and meeting process leadership. The next section provides the basic operational tactics needed to support the meeting process.

OPERATIONAL TACTICS TO SUPPORT THE MEETING PROCESS

Good meeting planning that produces an intuitive step-by-step process to achieve meeting outcomes is a powerful way to improve team performance with full participation of team members. Research shows that the more equal the participation in a group, the higher the collective intelligence of the group, and the higher the performance of the group.[6] Three ways for a team to support the meeting process are documentation, focus, and work with an external facilitator.

Many organizations use documentation to improve individual employee performance, so it is logical that documentation can be used to improve team performance too. Managers can use regular documentation of employee performance to monitor employee progress against goals and support evidence-based performance ranking. A manager who practices regular documentation of an employee's progress against goals can identify and address performance problems and barriers to performance as they occur. The earlier a limitation to performance is identified, the more options are available to address the limitation. Similarly, documentation of team meetings is a way to monitor progress against goals and identify limitations to group and individual team member performance.

A team leader can use a simple "minutes" template to take notes during a meeting or to delegate note taking to someone else during the meeting. The minutes template should have areas to capture the team name, the date and time of the meeting, notes for each agenda item, decisions made by the team, the consensus process used to make each team decision, "parking lot" items, and action items. A parking lot item is a topic or idea brought up by a team member that does not fit with the agenda item under discussion but will be reviewed later. An action item is a task that specifies who, what, and when for something that needs to be completed outside the team meeting. The assigned note taker can read the decisions made and action items created at the end of the meeting to check for accuracy. The team leader or a delegate types up the notes as minutes of the meeting for distribution to members to review before the next team meeting. I recommend having an agreed-to schedule for when minutes will be distributed to members after the meeting so there is adequate time for members to review them before the next meeting. For long meetings or meetings including sensitive information, the team leader can create a separate one-page executive summary of meeting highlights from the minutes for members and other stakeholders.

A meeting agenda is a form of documentation that occurs before a team meeting. An agenda helps team members prepare for a meeting and focus their attention during the meeting on the process and content needed to achieve meeting outcomes. A high-performance agenda is a detailed agenda based on a well-constructed meeting purpose, meeting objectives, and meeting outcomes. Such an agenda captures the preparation, content, process, and logistical details needed to produce the meeting outcomes. A sample high-performance team agenda for a kick-off meeting is provided here and can be customized for other types of meetings.

SAMPLE HIGH-PERFORMANCE TEAM AGENDA

Header

[TEAM NAME] Kick-Off Meeting

[DATE of Meeting]; [TIME of Meeting, TIME ZONE]

[LOCATION for Meeting] [DIAL-IN, LINK INFORMATION if applicable]

Proposed Meeting Objectives:
- Identify participant talents relevant to this team in order to streamline work going forward
- Review the Team Charter and Governance Plan in order to best meet the needs of the greater organization
- Identify the most important agenda items going forward in order to make best use of our limited time together

Proposed Agenda

SAMPLE HIGH-PERFORMANCE TEAM AGENDA

Topic, Time, Lead	Preparation	Process	Resources, Supplies
1. Gifts and Hook Exercise Time: 1:00–1:30 pm Purpose: Identify Participant Talents for Team's Work Lead: Team Leader	None	Welcome and explain purpose of Team (5 min) Explain exercise (3 min) Do exercise (15 min) Categorize and comment on input (5 min) Share next step (create resource off-line to inform work going forward, 2 min)	3 Slides (purpose, gifts and hooks, next step) Sticky note pads, pens Flipchart pad and stand Markers (to label flipchart sheets)
2. Input on Draft Committee Charter Time: 1:30–2:15 pm Purpose: Participant Input on Team Charter Lead: External Facilitator	Get input on the draft Team Charter from stakeholders that the team member represents	Identify advantages (2 min alone and then 8 more min as a group) Identify limitations as "how to" statements (2 min alone and then 8 more min as a group) Identify unique and valuable attributes (5 min as a group) Pick a limitation and generate ways to address (5 min) Repeat for additional limitations as time permits (15 min)	Draft Team Charter Sticky note pads and pens Flipchart stand and pad Markers (to label flipchart sheets)
3. Input on Draft Governance Plan Time: 2:15–3:00 pm	None	Same purpose and process as for Agenda Item 2 only now for the Draft Governance Plan	Draft Governance Plan

Topic, Time, Lead	Preparation	Process	Resources, Supplies
4. Networking Break Time: 3:00–3:15 pm	None	Informal time for brains to rest and for networking	Refreshments
5. Future Agenda Items Time: 3:15–3:45 pm Purpose: Identify Future Committee Topics Lead: Team Leader	None	Participants review the draft list Answer questions about the list and capture additions Pass out dots to prioritize the agenda items on the list	Draft list of future agenda items on a flipchart Dots for voting
6. Meeting Evaluation Time: 3:45–4:00 pm Purpose: Continually Improve Our Effectiveness as a Committee Lead: Team Leader	None	Ask participants to capture at least one benefit on a sticky note and at least one concern on a sticky note. (5 min) Ask for a volunteer to share their benefit(s) and concern(s). After they share, ask them to post on flipchart. (1 min) Go around the room for input on benefit(s) and concern(s) from each participant. (9 min)	Sticky note pads and pens Flipchart stand and pad Markers (to label flipchart sheets)

The sample high-performance team agenda includes an exercise for team members to provide input on a draft team charter and on a draft governance plan. A team charter is focused on the inner workings of a team to achieve the team goal, whereas a governance plan is focused on the external interactions needed to achieve the goal. Governance is a team's authority to take actions and develop policies and guidelines that impact other teams. A governance plan is needed when the work of a team impacts or needs to be coordinated with the work of other teams in the organization. For example, I wrote a governance plan to guide needed interactions by a Corporate Sustainability Community Council with the Health, Safety and Environmental (HSE) Community Council, the Human Resources Community Council, the Communications Community Council, and the Compliance Officers Community Council. CSCC shared the governance plan with the other community councils for their input and approval. The CSCC's governance plan included the following:

- Guiding principles for CSCC's interactions with other teams
- Scope and interfaces of CSCC's governance role
- In-scope and out-of-scope governance activities for CSCC
- Key activities and deliverables for CSCC's governance role
- Roles and responsibilities of each CSCC member
- Ratification of the governance plan by CSCC members

The elements of CSCC's governance plan can be customized to other teams as needed. Resources on governance charters also can be consulted to address a team's governance planning needs.[7]

Creating a team charter and ratifying a governance plan are two tactics to help a team focus on the meeting process needed to achieve their goals. Three more sample tactics to improve focus in support of meeting process are using barters, starters, and enders. Examples of a barter, a starter, and an ender to support meeting process are as follows.

A sample barter is a consent agenda. Such an agenda requires team members to address routine agenda items before a team meeting and, in exchange, time is freed up at the meeting for more strategic agenda items. A consent agenda is the prework that members are asked to do and is formatted as a series of tabs with a table of contents on the first page. Each tab is a document that is either informational, such as a progress report on deliverables, or needs approval, such as a fleshed-out project proposal that was an idea from the last meeting. One of the tabs of a consent agenda could be the minutes from the last meeting needing approval. The consent agenda is sent to members well ahead of the team meeting to give members time to read and reflect on informational items and perform due diligence needed for approval items. The agenda for the next meeting includes an agenda item called a consent agenda. The time allotted for the consent agenda enables a brief review of each tab to address questions and capture action items and decisions as warranted. The time saved on routine items using a consent agenda is applied to more strategic topics for team discussion and action planning.

A starter provides an opportunity to get team members interacting as soon as possible in a way that is relevant to or will help get participants in the right frame of mind for the main purpose of the meeting. A sample starter to improve team performance through focus is called "Seeing the Forest Through the Trees." This starter is effective for a meeting focused on setting high-level targets for a program.

SEEING THE FOREST THROUGH THE TREES STARTER

1. The team leader gives team members time to write down the first ten things that come to their minds on what they need or want to do from an individual perspective. No rules or restrictions are imposed. For example, the ten things could be from their professional life, from their personal life, or from a mixture of both.
2. The team leader displays the following table on a screen or provides the table as a handout and instructs team members to assign a letter or number from this table to

each of the ten things on their list. Members are to select
the letter or number that best characterizes the item in
terms of people impacted (rows) and the temporal scope
of the impact (columns).

	Tomorrow	Next Week	Sometime This Year	Sometime in My Life	Sometime in My Children's Lives
Colleagues	A	G	M	S	Y
Business Partners	B	H	N	T	Z
Family and/or Friends	C	I	O	U	1
City or Region	D	J	P	V	2
Country or Ethnic Group	E	K	Q	W	3
World	F	L	R	X	4

See the Forest through the Trees Table

3. The team leader sketches the table on a flipchart for tal-
   lying while team members complete the assignment exercise for their lists of ten things.
4. The team leader goes around the room and asks each
   team member to share their assignments (not the actual
   item on the list, only the letter or number assigned from
   the preceding table) and keeps tally on a flipchart. The
   leader checks that the tally adds up to ten times the number of members participating.
5. The result of the tally indicates the current scope of team
   members' thinking going into the meeting and a point
   of comparison to where the scope of members' thinking

needs to be for the meeting. The team leader specifies the letter(s) and number(s) of the scope of thinking needed for one or more of the current meeting's objectives or agenda items.

An ender provides an opportunity to end a meeting with inter-action and learn from what went well and what didn't go so well in the meeting so the next meeting can be even better. A sample ender to improve team performance through focus is called "Benefits and Concer   close every team meeting.

ERNS ENDER

1.   genda at the start of the
             nefits and concerns exer-

2.   member to write down one benefit and one concern they experienced as a result of the meeting. The leader encourages members to write down multiple benefits and multiple concerns in case of duplicates but explains they will be asked to share only one benefit and one concern in the report-out. The leader asks if there are questions about the exercise and then addresses questions.
3. The team leader provides enough time for each team member to capture at least one benefit and one concern and then goes around the room so each participant can share one benefit and one concern (duplicates are okay).
4. The team leader or designated note taker records the ben-efits and concerns while they are being shared.

5. Once each team member has shared one benefit and one concern, the team leader explains that this input will be analyzed before the next meeting so the input can be factored into planning the next meeting. Specifically, the leader will try to preserve the benefits shared and address the concerns raised in planning the next meeting.

A final tactic to help a team with meeting planning and meeting process is for a team leader to work with a facilitator. The team leader can hire a Certified Professional Facilitator (CPF),[8] can hire a consultant who has experience facilitating, or can contact the human resources department at their organization to find an internal facilitator. The leader or the team can prepare for their first interaction with the facilitator by answering a series of questions for a group task they need help with completing. The following questions are based on my experience working with clients as a CPF, but there may be more or different questions for your situation and needs. The leader may wish to create a first draft of answers and then seek input and comments from team members. The leader first identifies and documents the group task with as much detail as possible for working with the designated facilitator. Next, they document a first draft of answers relative to that group task for the following questions or their customized list of questions with as much detail as possible:

- What different perspectives would most benefit this group task?
- What types of expertise and knowledge would most benefit this group task?
- What parts of the group task are most important to address?
- What parts of the group task are least important to address?
- How is the group task linked to the strategic priorities of the team leader, team, or organization?

- Imagine the meeting to do the group task has occurred and you are really pleased with how things went. What does that success look like? What made you so pleased?
- What has been tried before to address this group task and what happened?
- How is what you want to create from this group task different from what you have now?
- Are you looking to improve current approaches and systems or create new or different ones with this group task?

The team leader may seek input from team members on the draft answers. The final step is for the leader to meet with the facilitator and discuss how to tackle the group task. The collaboration between the leader and facilitator is important to give the facilitator credibility with members and to ensure the facilitator's plans will meet the most pressing needs of the team. However, finding or hiring a facilitator is not always an option for a team, so the next section explores the science of engagement and examples of participative tactics used by facilitators. These samples tactics include those for consensus and implementation in teams.

OPERATIONAL TACTICS TO INCREASE TEAM MEMBER PARTICIPATION

Team member participation begins with engaging the members. Engagement is about getting and holding the attention of one or more other people. Scientists understand the limitations of the brain when it comes to holding attention and how the brain is wired to pay attention. For example, our brain is designed to focus our attention for up to twenty minutes at a time if there are no distractions.[9] Further, there is no such thing as multitasking because while the brain can switch between tasks at breakneck speed, it can pay attention to only one task at a time for most projects. Adding insult to injury, there is a cognitive performance cost associated with switching between cognitive tasks.[10] In fact, trying to multitask has been shown to degrade the ability to focus attention in the future.[11] Finally, our brains evolved to pay automatic and nonconscious attention in ways that increase the likelihood of our survival. Research has identified eight types of stimuli important to our survival based on evolution and that are still wired into our brains today.

The first stimulus for attention is people and especially faces. Research has shown that people can detect changes in faces more readily than changes in objects.[12] The second stimulus is animals, which can be sources of threat or reward when it comes to our well-being[13]—I don't know about you, but I can't resist a funny cat video. The third stimulus is salience in visual attributes like color, orientation, size, shape, and motion. Our brain is especially sensitive to pattern interruptions like "which one of these does not look like the other" from *Sesame Street*. Salience in color can indicate food like berries on a bush while salience in motion can indicate a predator like a black bear moving in a dark forest (both of which I have witnessed at my home in Vermont). The fourth stimulus is spatial cues like the direction of eye gaze and other directional cues like pointing. Eye gaze not only helps identify emotions and objects but also can indicate social status.[14] The fifth stimulus is emotional arousal and especially high-arousal emotions like anger, fear, and excitement because these emotions can indicate a threat or reward that impacts us.[15] The sixth stimulus is relevance to a goal that team members care about because achieving a goal is rewarding. The seventh stimulus is unpredictability because certainty is a shared social need.[16] Finally, the eighth stimulus is me-relevance because we are more likely to pay attention when we can see the relevance to ourselves. In fact, self-projection is related to many different types of high-level thinking, and high-level thinking takes extreme engagement and focus.[17]

Team activities can be made more engaging by tapping into one or more of the eight types of stimuli that our brain has been wired to pay attention to for our well-being. For example, people making a presentation at a team meeting can draw on these stimuli to help engage team members with the content on their slides. Team leaders can come up with creative and fun ways to use one or more of these types of stimuli to regain attention when there has been a distraction in a meeting. I used to project a cute picture of my cat on the screen when side conversations started up during a meeting to regain focus on me, the team leader.

Six primary types of engagement activities help guide team members to achieve meeting outcomes: generating ideas, prioritizing, setting levels, taking action, building trust, and building understanding. There are many different ways to practice these six types of engagement activities. The best way to practice an engagement activity in a team meeting will depend on the meeting purpose, objectives, outcomes, and the preferences of the person leading the activity. A sample participative tactic with context is provided for each type of engagement activity here.

One sample tactic for generating ideas is Around the World (AtW), which is a powerful technique when many people are interested in tackling several different problems. The idea of AtW is to divide the group among the different problems so there are two to seven people per problem. The groups are given time to tackle their assigned problem and document their ideas on sticky notes for others to read. When time is up for generating ideas, the groups rotate in one direction to consider the next problem. After a rotation, the group considers the ideas already generated on notes and then generates more ideas from their perspective and as triggered by the existing ideas. The rotation process continues until each group has the opportunity to provide input on each of the starting problems. AtW can be done using different rounds of rotation. For example, a first round of rotation can be used for independent work with no speaking between group members and a second round of rotation for interdependent work with discussion to build off one another's thinking.

A sample tactic for prioritizing is to use an evaluation matrix. Prioritization is a form of consensus focused on processing a collection of ideas or options as a next step toward taking action. An evaluation matrix has one axis for ease of implementation and another axis for the degree of impact. The two axes create four quadrants as follows: the upper-right quadrant for high-impact ideas that can be easily implemented, the upper-left quadrant for high-impact ideas that are challenging to implement, the lower-right quadrant for low- to medium-impact ideas that can be easily implemented, and the lower-left quadrant for low- to medium-impact ideas that are challenging to implement. Each option or idea under consideration must be placed in one of the four quadrants. The quadrants are not meant to be graphs, so it is not necessary to prioritize the ideas or options within a quadrant. Also, no ideas or options are allowed on the lines between quadrants because prioritization is about making decisions and sitting on the fence is not a decision. The options or ideas in the upper-right quadrant of the evaluation matrix are the best candidates for implementation.

A sample tactic for setting levels is an introvert moment.[18] Level setting is about removing sources of status advantage across team members and is particularly helpful when a team is meeting for the first time or when known status differences are present in a team. In an introvert moment, participants are given several minutes to capture insights based on content presented. After participants are done working alone to capture their insights, they share those insights with the group. This tactic helps bring out all perspectives without status differences getting in the way and helps introverts perform well among extroverts. This tactic can be used to provide a content basis to make a decision, solve a problem, or develop an action plan relevant to the context.

A sample tactic for taking action is proposed project planning (P3). The P3 tactic is designed to navigate around the natural tendency for negativity bias.[19] Negativity bias can cause team members to focus first on why a proposed project will not work, which can frustrate others who disagree and then degrade to unproductive conflict. Strong emotions caused by unproductive conflict are a barrier to the creativity and problem solving needed to overcome barriers to project implementation. The P3 tactic focuses first on the potential advantages of a proposed project to keep negative feelings at bay before considering limitations and ways to overcome limitations. This tactic provides a path for implementation of a project idea or concept.

PROPOSED PROJECT PLANNING (P3)

1. A group of three to seven people identifies a proposed project and writes down a description of the proposed project with as much detail as possible.

2. The group lists the advantages and benefits of implementing the proposed project without worrying about the challenges to or costs of implementation. The group considers: "If this proposed project is successfully implemented, then what are the potential advantages and benefits to those impacted and to the organization(s) impacted?" Group members list all the possible advantages and benefits that they can identify.

3. Group members list the limitations and concerns they have about the proposed project in the form of problem

statements. These statements must start with "How to," "In what ways might," or "How might." Using the proper format to list limitations and concerns ensures that the group is focused on identifying problems and not solutions, which comes later. The group considers: "What barriers and limitations are there to implementing this proposed project? What challenges are associated with the proposed proj

4. The group sele_____ ___ ___ ____ _imitation or concern about the propose_____ _____ generated in step 3. They the_____ ___ _____ __ that is the largest po_____ __ __ _ ___ ____ __ ___ proposed proj___

5. T___ ____ ___ _____ ____ __ ___ __ng the selected limit_____ ____ __ __ __ orm of a problem statement __ _____ _____ ___ ___deas are listed. Time permitting, the ____ _____ _____ steps 4 and 5 for additional limitations an____ ____.

6. The group writes down w__ _t is compelling about implementing the proposed project.

7. The group writes down a list of starting actions that could be taken to implement the proposed project that take into account overcoming limitations and concerns in the form of high-level milestones. The starting actions need to describe "what," "when," and "by whom."

A sample tactic for building trust in a large group of twenty-four or more people is brief encounters.[20] In this technique, each participant comes up with an important question they want help with from the people in the room. Each participant needs to come up with one question that if answered, would help them to improve in some way. The objective of the exercise is for participants to talk to as many people as they can in the time allotted. The format for each interaction is as follows: Person A asks their question, Person B answers, Person A says thank you, Person B asks their question, Person A answers, and then Person B says thank you. Next, Person A and Person B find a different person to repeat the interaction with. Participants are told that it is okay to not have an answer and, when stumped, to think of resources to share or ask for clarification of the question. This technique can be a powerful tool as a precursor to a networking opportunity for a large group.

A sample tactic for the final category of building understanding is a team process to clarify action items. Clarifying action items is one way to improve the completion of action items between team meetings. The team leader reserves time at the end of the meeting to do an exercise that promotes clarity and doability of action items. The leader can use a worksheet for this exercise that has a blank table with several rows and three columns. The first column is a description of the action item, the second column is for why the action item is important to the team's goals, and the third column is for resources needed for the action item. The worksheet should have space at the bottom for insights and comments from filling in the action point table. The leader hands out the action point table worksheets and reads the action items from the meeting so team members can fill in their assigned action items as rows in the first column of the table. Members are then given time (five to ten minutes) to fill in the second and third columns of the table for their action items and to capture insights and comments at the bottom of the worksheet. When members are ready, the leader goes around the room asking for a three- to five-minute report-out based on the exercise. The leader addresses questions and misunderstandings and changes action items or who is assigned as appropriate. The leader also needs to remember that it is more important to get assigned action items completed than it is to get all action items assigned.

A facilitator not only provides and leads participative activities to achieve meeting outcomes but also manages disruptive behavior in the meeting as needed. The next section provides some tips for managing disruptive behavior in a meeting.

OPERATIONAL TACTICS TO MANAGE DISRUPTION

Chemical engineers learn there are both minor and major disruptions to a manufacturing operation designed to make a specific product. For example, a minor disruption to a manufacturing operation to make toilet paper would reduce the number of toilet paper rolls being made but not the quality of the toilet paper. Similarly, a minor disruption for a meeting means lower efficiency in achieving meeting outcomes. A major disruption to a plant making toilet paper would result in discolored toilet paper that couldn't be sold or would stop the production of toilet paper altogether. Likewise, a major disruption for a meeting means the quality of meeting outcomes is unacceptable or no meeting outcomes are being produced.

Minor disruptions to a manufacturing operation can be caused by a change in a raw material supplier, a new operator who changes an equipment setting, or a mistake in equipment maintenance. Similarly, minor disruptions to a meeting can be caused by a new team member, a change in team process from what is expected, or a change in a member's behavior from what is expected. Small changes in manufacturing or team operations can produce minor disruptions to outputs. Minor disruptions to team meetings were addressed in chapter 4 on team composition for changes in team membership and in chapter 3 on team leadership for managing negative feelings expressed by members.

Major disruptions to a manufacturing operation can be caused by natural disasters, like a hurricane, and man-made disasters, like sabotage by a disgruntled employee. Major disruptions to a meeting can also be caused by natural and man-made disasters. I remember being in a meeting that quickly ended when news of an airplane crashing into one of the World Trade Center buildings in New York City broke on television. A bad snowstorm can also break up a meeting as people worry about getting home safely. But the most common cause of a major disruption to a meeting is unproductive conflict that leads to silence or violence behavior by one or more team members.

Productive conflict in a team happens when conflict leads to deeper thinking and learning by team members.[21] Unproductive conflict happens when conflict leads to negative feelings and defensive or aggressive behavior that escalates the conflict and distracts members.[22] Productive conflict supports a team meeting when it is timely and relevant. It can also be managed with a "parking lot" when it is not timely or when it is irrelevant to the meeting task at hand. As noted previously, a parking lot is a technique to capture input that is irrelevant in the moment but that can be reviewed later for follow-up. Unproductive conflict is disruptive to a team meeting and must be addressed. There are both proactive and reactive ways to manage unproductive conflict that is disruptive to a meeting.

A proactive way to manage unproductive conflict is to use techniques that help team members meet their social needs. For example, establishing behavioral norms in a meeting helps eliminate uncertainty and promote fairness for members. Norms can be customized to a team or to a meeting. Following is a sample list of norms I have used when creativity is important in a team meeting. The content in parentheses is how I would explain and justify the use of the norm to meeting participants.

SAMPLE TEAM NORMS TO SUPPORT CREATIVITY

- What is discussed stays in the room (this norm is important because this session addresses an unexplored topic and participants need to feel safe to share their thoughts).
- What could be helpful to action needed must get captured on a sticky note or flipchart page (this norm is important because the record of this session will be based only on what is captured in writing on sticky notes and flipchart pages).
- Trust the process (this norm recognizes that every person has the ability to be creative and that the process being used here has been designed to maximize creativity).
- Be open to different perspectives (this norm is important because there is not enough time for introductions, so participants will get to know each other through working together; therefore, high trust and openness will be needed).
- Try a relaxed state of attention for brainstorming on your own (this norm is based on the science of insight, which finds that an insight is most likely when you are in a relaxed state of attention with your focus off the problem).

A team leader or third-party facilitator can take steps to manage unproductive conflict in preparation for a team meeting. For example, the leader or facilitator can identify status differences among team members such as asymmetries in knowledge or recent changes in jobs. Then the planning for the meeting can take into account how these status differences might lead to dysfunction. Further, the leader or facilitator can look for sources of uncertainty for members. Uncertainty can cause a member to act out, so eliminating sources of uncertainty can avoid this source of dysfunction. Finally, the leader or facilitator can survey members ahead of time to explore how the planned content might trigger concerns and how triggered concerns could be alleviated.

Unfortunately, team leaders or third-party facilitators can't anticipate all sources of conflict before a meeting, so they need to know how to manage nonproductive conflict as it arises. Nonproductive conflict is managed by determining which of the three underlying causes of conflict exists. One underlying cause of conflict is different sources of information. To test for this cause, the parties involved in the conflict are asked to explain the information on which their position is based. If there is a difference in sources of information, then the conflict is resolved by better understanding these differences and taking into account the new information. A second underlying cause of conflict is different values or experiences. To test for this cause, the parties involved in the conflict are asked to explain why they are taking their position. This type of conflict is resolved by better understanding the differences in values and experiences related to the topic and taking into account the new perspectives. The final underlying cause of conflict is external factors like personality differences, past history, or other outside factors that lead to interpersonal problems. The best way to handle a conflict based on an external factor is to elevate the conflict to a higher authority outside the meeting to resolve the conflict after the meeting.

Team operation is about the process to achieve meeting outcomes and is often second fiddle to the content and expertise needed for a meeting. The neglect of team operation is understandable because the character and competence that build effective team leaders do not guarantee the team leader will have the skills needed for process facilitation.

This chapter provided tactics that team leaders can use to improve meeting planning, team member engagement, consensus, and implementation. Leaders can also take Fulcrum's Facilitation

Assessment to evaluate and learn how to improve upon facilitation skills. The next chapter takes a deeper dive into designing meetings that matter.

Here are some reflection exercises and questions for this chapter on team operation to enhance learning:

- What aspects of engaging others most resonated with you and why?
- What new ideas did you get for running meetings that you would like to try and why?
- In what ways might you improve your approach to prepare for a meeting you are leading? Jot down all the ideas you can think of and then pick the top one or two that you would like to try at your next meeting.

CHAPTER 7

Troubleshooting Meeting Design

The design of a meeting can help or hurt its outcomes. For example, drilling down on one possible solution to a problem without considering and ranking a range of possible solutions may produce suboptimal outcomes. Troubleshooting meeting design helps ensure that the design of a meeting helps maximize the quality of its outcomes.

Success in meeting design not only produces high-quality outcomes but also is measured by meeting participants. Participants get energized by a great meeting design because their time and intellect get put to good use. However, participants get disappointed by a poor meeting design because they feel that their time and intellect were wasted in the meeting. A meeting designer, like a product designer, can influence success by their choice of design process. For example, industrial designers have learned that a product designed to user-specified needs will be less successful in the marketplace than a product based on needs uncovered when designers observe users. All other things being equal, the process used to design a meeting can make the difference between energized and disappointed participants at the end of the meeting. Troubleshooting meeting design to maximize quality of outcomes and the experiences of participants means improving the meeting design process.

I discovered the strong influence of process on outcomes as a freshman at Bucknell University in my first chemical engineering class called Mass Balances. This course taught me that tweaking a chemical process can change the outputs you get from the same inputs, just like changing how you combine the same ingredients in baking can impact the output. I learned from my father-in-law, who learned from his mother, that the secret to getting a flaky pie crust is in how much you work the dough. The more you work the dough, the less flaky the resulting pie crust. For a flaky pie crust, I learned to combine the ingredients with as little mixing as possible and roll out the dough with as little contact with the rolling pin as possible. My chemical engineering training and failed pie baking experiences exposed me to the world of "how" in a world I had viewed as dominated by "whats."

This chapter is about the "whats" of meeting design but focuses on the "how" also because the "how" is what will determine success or failure. Examples of "whats" for meeting design are content to present or share in the meeting, input needed from meeting participants, time available to meet, and location or technology to hold the meeting. In contrast, examples of "hows" for meeting design are envisioning the steps to produce needed change, articulating the input participants must provide, determining the ways in which participants need to interact with content and each other to produce the outcomes, and specifying supplies to enable participants to best interact with content and each other. It is natural for professionals to focus on the "whats" of meeting design because they use their "whats" of perspective and expertise to solve a problem or enable action in a meeting. Many participants aren't used to or aren't happy about paying attention to meeting process, but it is the "how" of meeting design that can put participant perspectives and expertise to best use. Mark Alan Hughes, Director of the Kleinman Center for Energy Policy at the University of Pennsylvania, put his reservations about meeting process this way: "Many participants, myself included, [are] academics who are highly resistant to be facilitated or subjected to any other obvious intervention in their own reflections and debates. But Val always manages to get through the process with no one the worse for wear and improves the outcomes for all." I made Mark a true believer in the power of a well-designed process to improve meeting outcomes.

Meeting design is related to but different from team operation. The difference between team operation and meeting design is like the difference between baking utensils and a recipe for a pie. Making a pie takes combining the right ingredients using the right sequence of baking utensils just like producing meeting outcomes takes the right participants using the right sequence of team operations. Each baking utensil in making a pie is selected from a range of possibilities. For example, if you need to combine ingredients, then you can choose a whip, a fork, a wooden spoon, an electric blender, or your hands, depending on the properties of the ingredients and the impact on the outcome. Each team operation in a meeting can also be selected from a range of possibilities. For example, leaders can get input from participants by calling on people who raise their hands, going around the room, using unstructured brainstorming, or using structured brainstorming around a specific problem with a specific format for input. Teams can get into trouble when their operations limit meeting outcomes. Meeting design provides a deliberate way to select team operations that maximize meeting outcomes.

Meeting design, like baking a pie, is at its best when it incorporates both strategic and tactical elements. Specifically, baking a pie is more strategic than just choosing the baking utensils and the sequence of using those utensils to produce the pie. For example, the best bakers anticipate problems, such as how to prevent a soggy pie bottom for a particular filling. This type of strategic decision needs to be made before drilling down to other tactical details like how long to bake the pie after it is assembled because a pre-bake may be needed before assembly. Similarly, meeting designers have learned to consider the alignment of meeting outcomes with organizational goals and strategy before drilling down to tactical details.

Meeting design is the path to convert team inputs to team outputs just as a recipe is the path to convert ingredients to baked goods. The best meeting designs focus on meeting outcomes within a bigger strategic context while tending to every detail of meeting process. Strategic context is important when your team serves a competitive role for the organization, such as differentiating a new product from other suppliers.[1] Strategic context is also important to pursue and achieve results that will be most valued by the organization. This type of context comes from a compelling vision that guides and focuses teamwork toward actions that otherwise would not be undertaken. A compelling vision is a picture of the future beyond what others are doing. For example, compelling visions can be born out of one or more of the following circumstances:

- things people say have been tried in the past,
- things that are the opposite of what your peers are doing,
- things perceived to be controversial, or
- things perceived to be too difficult or too complex to do.

The compelling vision that powered a forum to support my new role as head of sustainability for a leading global chemicals and pharmaceuticals company was to be a sustainability leader in North America. Many viewed this vision as too difficult because of how far behind we were from our competitors on taking action to support sustainable development at the time. But the forum ended up being the first step toward future recognition and rewards for our organization in the sustainability space. Meetings that matter are well-designed meetings that capture the imagination and full participation by all present, which is not always easy.

SYMPTOMS OF MEETING DESIGN PROBLEMS

The primary symptom of a meeting design problem is lack of commitment by team members during and following the meeting. Members lack commitment when they are not convinced the team is on the right path. Commitment is a precious and powerful human trait that is necessary for getting high-quality work done in a team.

Team members provide clues of their lack of commitment when they are indifferent, complain, avoid engagement, behave with hostility, or express disagreement.[2] An example of indifference is a member checking emails or their phone during a meeting. An example of complaining is a member pointing out what is wrong without a suggestion or recommendation on how to fix the issue. Avoiding engagement is prompted by doubt of success or fear of risks such as a member saying, "I'm not sure that will work." Hostile behavior is being rude or threatening in order to stop a course of action in a team meeting, such as a member saying, "You don't have the authority to do that." Disagreement is challenging an idea or course of action with an explanation, such as a member saying "Yes, but . . ."

The solution to lack of commitment is persuasion, which uses social interaction to change another person's beliefs, attitudes, or behaviors in support of the meeting design. Persuasion is distinct from manipulation, which is using social interaction to get what you want by limiting the free will of another person. Persuasion to increase commitment does not limit the free will of another person in changing their thinking and actions. A lack of commitment is addressed with persuasion that removes the boredom, frustration, fear, anger, or disagreement experienced by another person. Neuroscientists have found that persuasion is most effective when the parts of the brain associated with social processing are activated.[3] We activate social processing in our brain when we are interested in learning about another person. Thus, persuasion works best when both parties are interested in learning more about each other.

Persuasion is important to meeting design when the meeting designer does not have the authority to implement the design of their choosing. The meeting designer might be a third-party facilitator hired by a team leader or recruited from another part of the organization. They might be a subordinate to a manager or executive who will be leading or participating in the meeting. The rest of this section provides persuasion tactics for meeting designers who need the support of others to implement their design ideas and design input. These persuasion tactics can also be used by the person running the meeting to gain commitment of meeting participants.

One persuasion tactic is to get the other person interested in learning more about you before asking them to support your meeting design. You can trigger another person's interest in learning more about you by identifying something you have in common. For example, you can share random information about your personal, professional, and social interests and see which topics capture the attention and interest of the other person. I recently connected with a finance major on an airplane over a shared interest in intangible capital. But you should be careful to avoid words and phrases that can trigger divisiveness like *climate change, immigration,* and *abortion.* Once you bond with another person on a shared interest, you are more likely to persuade the other person.

A second persuasion tactic is to ascertain how the other person likes to think and then draw upon that type of thinking to support your meeting design.[4] For example, you can ask the other person what they are most excited about working on right now or to describe a work accomplishment they are most proud of and why. I would answer that I am most excited about writing this book because it is a new and challenging experience for me. Next, you should listen for clues in their answer for their preferred problem-solving style, such as process-focused, analytical, idea-focused, or relationship-focused. For example, my answer about the book shows that I am idea-focused. Finally, you should position your meeting design to draw upon their preferred approach to problem solving. So you could point out how your meeting design will promote new ideas or approaches, and I would gladly engage to learn more.

A final persuasion tactic is to express conviction for your meeting design while inviting the other person to collaborate. A format to try for this third method is as follows:

- First, express your conviction: "I believe . . ." (or I am sure . . ., convinced . . ., certain . . ., and so on)
- Second, invite the other person's input: "Let's discuss . . ."
- Third, state the joint purpose such as a decision to be made: "so that we can . . . "

Here is an example of using this tactic to persuade a team leader to use an interactive approach for a meeting on increasing gender diversity in leadership: "I believe there are systemic problems causing barriers to gender diversity in leadership because these barriers have persisted for the last thirty years I have worked in a corporate environment. Let's discuss ways to uncover the systemic problems causing a lack of gender diversity in leadership so that we can decide how to engage participants in proposing solutions to these problems." This tactic worked to convince the team leader to consider an interactive approach to the meeting.

To create a meeting design worthy of persuading others to support, you can start with the principles of good meeting design discussed in the next section.

PRINCIPLES OF GOOD MEETING DESIGN

A team meeting is complex by nature because the actions and thoughts of other people are difficult to predict. Scientists who study complexity find that there are principles that can predict if a system will produce constructive or destructive outcomes. Principles are system rules that are among the top five ways to leverage a system for constructive outcomes.[5] Meeting design also has a set of principles to help ensure desired outcomes.

Guiding principles help frame and focus a task or activity on what is most important when there are several potential issues and possibilities. You can think of guiding principles as a checklist to ensure you do a high-quality job on a task that takes consideration of more variables than you can keep in your head at any one time. The guiding principles shared here for meeting design are based on my experience leading team meetings and serving as a third-party facilitator but may need to be customized for your preferences and needs.

The first of five principles for good meeting design is to use leadership vision to inform clear end goals. Leadership vision can come from different sources including the team leader, a third-party facilitator, and a team member. Leadership vision can also come from one or more of the organization's executives or from making a connection between the organization's strategy and the team's charter. The end goals for the meeting need to be understandable with a clear connection to the leadership vision. For example, a facilitation client wanted a workshop to normalize gender contributions at home and at work. The leadership vision from the organization's website was to represent diversity and inclusion in the sciences. The workshop goal became to increase female participation at scientific conferences and in leadership positions so that the benefits of gender diversity to science and organizational performance are realized. If you ask, "Why normalize gender contributions at home and at work?" then one answer is to realize the benefits of gender diversity to science and organizations. Leadership vision directs the meeting outcome toward a meaningful "why."

The second principle for good meeting design is to use a goal hierarchy to provide motivation and enable action. Research shows that structuring a goal to show the relationship between concrete activities and more abstract objectives enhances the likelihood of achieving that goal.[6] More abstract objectives speak to meaning such as values and the kind of organization or group you want to be in order to achieve success in the long term. Our brain is designed to be interested in things that are meaningful to us and rewarding to us in some way. To understand the more abstract objectives for a goal, ask why you want to achieve the goal to tease out the meaning. Keep asking why to move to higher levels of abstraction. For example, moving to higher levels of abstraction for the goal "normalize gender contributions at home and at work" can look like the following:

- Why normalize gender contributions at home and at work? Because responsibilities for women in the home keep them from putting the time in to advance in the workplace.
- Why do women need more time to advance in the workplace? Because women need to work harder than men to have the same advancement opportunities.
- Why do women need to work harder than men? Because women face performance barriers in the workplace that men don't face.
- Why do women face performance barriers that men don't face? Because there are fewer women in leadership positions to identify and remove performance barriers.

A goal at a higher level of abstraction for "normalize gender contributions at home and at work" would be "increase female participation in leadership positions."

The concrete activities for a goal enable action and are uncovered by asking how to achieve the goal. For example, moving to more concreteness for the goal "normalize gender contributions at home and at work" can look like the following:

- How would you normalize gender contributions at home and at work? You can normalize gender contributions at work by creating more career opportunities for women compared to men.
- How would you create more career opportunities for women? Select more female scientists to present research at conferences.
- How would you select more female scientists to present research at conferences? Keep track of the number of female versus male scientists presenting at conferences each year and set a goal to make this an equal number.

A goal at a lower level of abstraction for "normalize gender contributions at home and at work" would be "target sending equal numbers of men and women to be research presenters at conferences."

Goals at a higher level of abstraction are articulated by asking "why" and serve as a source of motivation for goal pursuit. Goals at a lower level of abstraction are obtained by asking "how" and enable action but can also identify barriers and problems. But asking "how else" when a barrier or problem is encountered in goal pursuit within the framework of the abstract objective provides ideas to overcome and move past roadblocks. Also, asking "why else" of the abstract version of the goals helps address motivation challenges in goal pursuit.

The third principle for good meeting design is to maximize value delivered from the meeting. Value is maximized by increasing the benefits to others, the efficiency of delivering those benefits, and the quality of those benefits.[7] So the meeting designer needs to identify the team's stakeholders, the benefits the meeting will deliver to those stakeholders, how to measure quality of those benefits, and how to achieve those benefits with efficiency. The team's stakeholders are the people most affected by the successful completion of the team's goals. For example, one facilitation client wanted input on their research programs from the people who would be using the research results. One of the outcomes defined for that meeting was for participants to understand how a research program would benefit them before providing input. The benefits of the meeting to stakeholders need to be reflected in the meeting outcomes. To deliver high-quality benefits, the meeting designer identifies the expertise, knowledge, and perspectives needed to deliver the benefits and how to access the relevant content and perspectives. Finally, efficiency in delivering benefits comes from facilitation experience. A meeting designer can develop facilitation experience through study and training as well as through learning from other more experienced facilitators.

The fourth principle for good meeting design is finding ways of accessing expertise, knowledge, and perspectives missing from team members but important to achieving meeting outcomes. A meeting designer can access content and perspective missing from participants in different ways. For example, a meeting designer can recruit ad hoc participants for the meeting to fill in content and perspective gaps. Alternatively, they can interview experts or those with different perspectives outside the meeting and use that content in the meeting design. Content can be used in different formats including video, graphic posters, infographics, and preread materials. For example, I prepared a couple of educational videos on a meeting topic for participants to watch before the meeting as background for one facilitation client.

The final principle for good meeting design is to ensure that process leadership and process expertise are accessible during the meeting. The meeting designer can provide detailed and tested process instructions to the team leader or assigned process leader. The designer can also serve as the facilitator to ensure that the meeting is conducted with the climate and process needed to achieve meeting objectives. Finally, the designer can recruit an external facilitator and work with them to ensure understanding of meeting objectives and troubleshoot ways to address unanticipated challenges in the meeting. A process expert like a Certified Professional Facilitator[8] is recommended to handle anticipated resistance from participants and other barriers to achieving meeting outcomes.

The five meeting design principles help frame a good meeting design process. The principles of using leadership vision to inform clear end goals and using a goal hierarchy to provide motivation and implementation guidance for goal pursuit are most helpful at the start of this process. The principle to maximize value delivered applies throughout the process. Finally, the principles to access missing knowledge, expertise, and perspectives and to have process leadership expertise in the meeting are most helpful toward the end of the meeting design process. The next section delves into the mechanics of meeting design.

COMPONENTS OF MEETING DESIGN

Meeting design is choosing the outcome types and what is needed to achieve those outcomes, factoring in available resources and the situation. It is like travel in that it is a plan to achieve predetermined goals. For example, when you have an opportunity to travel someplace new, you can plan an itinerary of what to do and see and then pack according to that itinerary, taking into account constraints and mishaps. Similarly, meeting design needs to take into account the supplies, logistics, and information needs to achieve planned outcomes within the conditions, constraints, and unplanned disruptions associated with the meeting.

Meeting design starts with the meeting outcomes just like travel starts with a destination. There are different types of meeting outcomes just as there are different types of travel destinations, such as beaches, mountains, rainforests, and cruises. The types of meeting outcomes include learning, identifying problems or opportunities, solving problems, enabling action, and making decisions. Enabling action can include building acceptance, establishing trust, ensuring understanding, framing possible problems, identifying possible opportunities, and creating an action plan. Here are some questions that can help a meeting designer isolate the primary types of meeting outcomes needed:

- Imagine that the meeting has already taken place and you are very happy with how things went. What happened to make you so happy?
- What do we need to learn in this meeting?
- Is this meeting about solving a specific problem or pursuing a specific opportunity?
- Is this meeting about identifying what the important problems or opportunities are?
- What does this meeting need to enable us to do? Build acceptance? Build trust? Build understanding? Frame possible problems? Identify top opportunities? Create an action plan? Make a decision?
- What decisions need to be made in this meeting? After this meeting? Before this meeting?

After the types of outcomes are identified for the meeting, the meeting designer needs to determine what is needed to achieve those outcomes. Six types of design considerations support achieving meeting outcomes:

- Gathering data for discovery
- Gathering data for understanding
- Analyzing application of data
- Generating ideas
- Prioritizing
- Planning action

A meeting designer can step through these design considerations one at a time for each meeting outcome to determine how to best use the meeting time.

An example to illustrate the use of a meeting outcome question and the list of design considerations for a meeting design is a consultation I did for a research institute to enable a request of project proposals for funding. I used the first outcome question of asking the client to imagine that the meeting had already occurred and that they are very happy with the results to reflect on what outcomes would make them happy. The client said that success was participants having identified cool and important technical problems and consensus of what industry wants. The type of outcome represented by "cool and important technical problems" is problem identification. The type of outcome represented by "consensus of what industry wants" is building acceptance to enable the action of issuing a request for project proposals.

The first design consideration for identifying "cool and important technical problems" is data gathering for discovery in support of this outcome. The client had already gathered data on research needs and had distilled the findings down into four different high-level operational areas. So the client checked off the first three design considerations of gathering data for discovery, gathering data for understanding, and analyzing application of data. The next design consideration on the list is generating ideas. Given the four different operational areas, the meeting could be designed for idea generation to find the best research problems to work on in each of these four operational areas. The client could provide background information for each operational area to establish common ground for the existing state of technology so that the problems identified would be future-looking. The client also could craft a statement to guide and trigger generation of the technical problems to address for each operational area. Participants could be assigned to an initial operational area and then could rotate through the different operational areas to build off each other's ideas and contribute to all areas. The next design consideration on the list is prioritization, which would also be needed to select the top technical problems from all those identified. For example, prioritization could be done using color-coded dot voting of the technical problems identified by idea generation. The color-coding would distinguish votes by industry, university, and government participants because the client specified consensus from industry as an important outcome. The final design consideration is planning the action, which ties into the second outcome of "consensus of what industry wants."

Let's revisit the list of design considerations for the "consensus of what industry wants" outcome. The first three design considerations are about gathering and analyzing data to support this outcome. In this case, the client had identified six technology thrust areas from analyzing data gathered on research needs. The idea generation and prioritization needed for this outcome are the top technical problems identified for the "cool and important technical problems" outcome. Thus, the design focus for the "consensus of what industry wants" outcome is action planning. Action planning could be achieved through worksheets to further define the top technical problems with respect to the six technology thrust areas. For example, participants could work in small groups according to technology thrust area to fill in worksheets specifying the industry applications, technical advances, research capabilities, and prototyping needs.

Sometimes it is relatively straightforward to put the components of meeting design together to achieve the meeting outcomes. The more concrete the meeting outcomes, the more straightforward it is to design the meeting. However, the more abstract the meeting outcomes, the more challenging it is to design the meeting. The next section provides an example of a more challenging meeting design.

EXAMPLE OF ADVANCED MEETING DESIGN

Advanced meeting design requires integrative planning that pulls together the components and principles of meeting design. One of the biggest challenges of planning is that it works in opposition to the way our brain is designed to work. Planning requires starting from the abstract and then determining the concrete steps needed. But our brain works by starting from the concrete and then moving toward the abstract as we are motivated to do so. For example, the first thing I notice when I look at a plaque on my desk is the color contrast between the off-white background and dark brown wood frame. Next, I notice that there are bluish-gray letters on the poster and that the letters form words centered on the plaque. The words read as follows: "Yesterday is already a dream, and tomorrow is only a vision; but today, well lived, makes every yesterday a dream of happiness and every tomorrow a vision of hope." Finally, I ask myself if I care what the words mean and I know that I do because I am interested in happiness and that word captures my attention. I think about the words and conclude that the message is that if I am happy today, then I will look on my past and toward my future with optimism. In looking at the plaque, my brain started with the most concrete information—contrasting colors—and then ended with the most abstract information—happiness breeds happiness. In contrast, meeting design starts with the most abstract information and ends with the most concrete information.

Advanced meeting design starts with critical thinking, including strategic thinking and problem solving. Critical thinking is the most abstract form of thinking. This type of thinking is needed to determine the meeting outcomes and the design considerations for a meeting. It is also needed to allocate time to the different group activities and to sequence the group activities to achieve meeting outcomes. Meeting designers need to convert this critical thinking into a clear step-by-step process, list of meeting supplies, and logistics needed to achieve the meeting outcomes.

In my experience, no two advanced meeting designs are identical. So rather than trying to provide a formula for advanced meeting design that would need to be customized, I am going to illustrate the key aspects of advanced meeting design with one of my favorite examples. At the end of the example, I will summarize the steps used to serve as a framework and starting point for other advanced meeting design needs.

My example of advanced meeting design was triggered by an interview with the CEO of a multinational chemical and pharmaceutical company. The CEO was interviewing me for a position to lead sustainability efforts for the company's North America operations. In the interview, the CEO challenged me to find the North America equivalent of sustainability projects that had recently been announced at our global headquarters in Europe. After our meeting, I did some critical thinking about the sample projects from Europe that the CEO mentioned. I asked myself: what makes these projects so impressive in the eyes of the CEO? I realized these projects were examples of technical innovation for a more sustainable world that implemented a technical idea to create value for both the company and society at large. The CEO also expressed the desire to differentiate our company as a leader in sustainability. I reasoned that a corporate sustainability leader needed to advance business goals while addressing sustainability challenges; otherwise, the sustainability effort would not be sustainable over time. This strategic thinking triggered the need to bring together business experts with sustainability experts to find projects with business attractiveness that would help put our company at the forefront of sustainable development in North America. I also reasoned that the first step to technology-driven innovation is to understand the critical unmet needs in the marketplace. Thus, leadership sustainability projects are found at the intersections of our technical and business competencies with possible solutions to critical unmet needs.

The critical thinking catalyzed by the CEO crystallized an idea to hold a workshop to identify the critical unmet needs for sustainability as a way to identify possible focal points for our North America strategy. Our company would benefit from this workshop by leveraging the collective brain power of experts from government, academia, and our company to identify possible focal points for sustainability projects. External participants in this workshop would benefit by being part of a diverse group of experts identifying a comprehensive list of unmet needs and opportunities for sustainability that would benefit from our technical investment.

The workshop idea needed to support technical innovation, so I needed to understand the current situation of technology-driven sustainability projects by us and our competitors in North America. The current situation would provide a benchmark that we would need to surpass in the workshop to be able to produce ideas that could differentiate us as a sustainability leader. One step was to identify and then interview our company's lobbyists in each of our business units who were focused on environmental and sustainability topics. Our lobbyists would be aware of top unmet needs and of what our company and our competitors were working on to address those needs. Another step was to interview the person who had recommended the head of sustainability position be created at our company. This person had pulled together a team that used situation assessment to show our company lagged our competitors in taking sustainability actions. A final step was to consult with a facilitation trainer on the workshop idea to get expert advice on what would be required to implement the idea. I was still early in my facilitation journey with only a handful of events under my belt that I had designed and facilitated myself. This practicing facilitation trainer had thousands of hours of experience. Together we envisioned a two-day event consisting of the following:

- half day for presentations to create a shared knowledge base,
- half day of facilitated divergent thinking to create a comprehensive list of unmet needs and opportunities for sustainability,
- half day of facilitated convergent thinking to develop the raw ideas into well-formulated needs and opportunities, and
- half day to formulate conclusions and next steps.

The workshop needed structure to guide group thinking toward unmet needs and opportunities most likely to fuel our company's sustainability leadership. So I needed to identify and understand strategic themes of most relevance to our company's competencies for the workshop. I put myself on a steep learning curve by going on an odyssey designed to learn from experts in the sustainability field. I attended four different sustainability events in the span of one month and transformed into a metaphorical sponge to absorb as much knowledge and expertise as I could. I also asked many questions of conference presenters and conference attendees to trigger thinking and insights relevant to my company's products and markets. Each morning of a given conference, I would think about and debrief what I had learned the day before to inform my learning and questions for the coming conference day. Learn, ask, and think are three of the eight practices to generate insights according to research.[9] Here are some sample insights from my learning odyssey:

- There are competing technologies to address sustainability needs, such as Jathropha versus perennial grasses as a new source of renewable energy that do not compete with food or animal feed supplies.
- It is most productive to collaborate with members of moderate nongovernmental organizations (NGOs) because they will be more future-looking than extremist NGOs looking to condemn current industry practices.
- A carbon lens creates new thinking and opportunities for new products.
- All companies learn that supply chain is a far larger source of their environmental footprint than their operations, which is why a view up and down the supply chain is important in sustainability.
- Life cycle assessment is a supply chain tool that can be used to find sustainability focal points for a product or process.

My learning odyssey enabled me to put together a workshop proposal that the CEO funded. The proposal included funds for professional facilitation so that I could be freed up to participate as a sustainability content expert in the workshop, dubbed the BASIN Workshop based on an acronym for B-company Advancing Sustainability through the Identification of Needs. Now it was time for high-level planning with the professional facilitation team so I could start the work needed to implement a top-notch workshop.

The first step of high-level planning was finalizing the strategic themes of most relevance to our company's businesses so I could target the most relevant external sustainability experts for participation in the workshop. The second step was developing selling points for the external sustainability experts to attend because I did not have budget to offset their travel costs or time commitment. The facilitator team and I brainstormed a list of selling points for each government, university, and NGO sustainability expert. The third and final step was identifying participants and recruiting them to participate in the workshop. We agreed to target no more than thirty-six participants total, so breakout groups across three professional facilitators would be twelve or fewer people. We also agreed to target at least nine external sustainability experts to have three per breakout group. Finally, we discussed giving voice to each external sustainability expert by asking them to write a one- to two-page white paper on their area of expertise as input for the workshop. The white paper was to discuss three to five topics to enable external sustainability experts to crystallize top priorities. In fact, the invitation to create a white paper could also serve as a selling point for the external expert to influence our company's direction for and investment in sustainability.

The final step to designing the BASIN Workshop was detailed meeting design with the professional facilitation team. We started with a high-level agenda for the two days as follows:

Day 1

9:30 a.m.	Coffee
10 a.m.	Welcome and Forum Overview
	• Developing a Shared Focus
	• Generating Session One
12:30 p.m.	Lunch with Assignment
	• Generating Session Two
	• Sorting Options—Focusing on Importance
6:00 p.m.	Close/Feedback
6:30 p.m.	Dinner

Day 2

7:30 a.m.   Breakfast

8:00 a.m.   Welcome Back—Getting Started
- Sorting Options—Focusing on Capability
- Selecting of Priority Recommendations
- Developing a Rationale for the Recommendations

12:30 p.m.   Lunch
- Group Presentations—Sharing Results
- Questions and Suggestions
- Feedback
- Next steps

3:30 p.m.   Close

Then we discussed the process behind each agenda item in detail to identify content, supply, and logistic needs. As part of this detailed planning, we decided to convert the white papers submitted by the external sustainability experts into graphic posters. The plan was to use the posters as an easily digestible format to be displayed in a separate room over lunch for a lunchtime work assignment. The posters were to be a surprise to participants and would be sent as thank-you gifts to the external sustainability experts following the workshop. The following is an excerpt from the detailed meeting design for opening the workshop as an example.

Timing: 10:00 to 10:45 a.m.
Flow of Activities:
Welcome, Purpose, Overview (Workshop Sponsor)
- Open with a welcome
- Introduce the topic, set the context and share Workshop purpose, deliverables
- Introduce CEO

Welcome Vision—importance (CEO)
- Importance to the company locally and regionally

*Fit to Global Strategy (Executive from
Global HQ in Europe) 5–10 mins*
- Corporate supports the Forum
- Importance to the company globally
- Global Sustainability Report

Outcome: People understand who is there, why we are here, the importance of the Workshop to the company's US operations and the strategic fit with the global strategy. They see the flow of the day.

Logistics/Materials: Flipcharts (FC): Purpose, deliverables, Agenda, Norms. Room set up in auditorium style with a podium for the CEO to speak and large screen for live video feed of global executive.

The steps taken for this example of advanced meeting design started from the abstract and ended with the concrete, as is the nature of planning. The five high-level steps illustrated in this example of advanced meeting planning are as follows:

1. Strategic thinking for the reason to have a meeting (most abstract)
2. Situation assessment to refine and crystallize meeting objectives
3. Learning odyssey in search of content and to fuel insight for how to achieve meeting objectives
4. High-level meeting design
5. Detailed meeting design (most concrete)

The participants and the CEO viewed this workshop as successful. It also paved the way for a sustainability strategy, sustainability goals, and a sustainability report for the company's North America operations. But one successful workshop is not enough to master the art of meeting design.

SYSTEM FOR MASTERING MEETING DESIGN

The more meetings I design, the more I appreciate all of the facets to and challenges of their design. My journey to advanced meeting design reminds me of my journey to becoming an expert downhill skier. All skiers, like all meeting designers, start out as beginners. Some never get past the beginner stage and the reasons vary as to why. Some beginner skiers get pushed too hard too soon and feel like a failure. Other beginner skiers feel a threat to their social needs for status, certainty, or autonomy, which can be threatened on skis until you are able to stop when you need to under different ski conditions. I remember my first time skiing with my husband in the White Mountains of New Hampshire, and I couldn't understand why there were times I could not stop and times I stopped for no reason. It turns out that I couldn't stop on patches of ice while patches of wet man-made snow made me stop on a dime. Nevertheless, my motivation and interest for skiing were driven by my husband's love of the sport and my interest to take on new physical challenges.

Those with the interest and motivation to get past the beginner phase to the intermediate phase have the skill to move on to expert skiing or meeting design. But not all intermediate skiers or meeting designers become advanced in their skills. Intermediate skiers who do not become advanced skiers don't take the risks needed for that transition. For example, you need to gain enough speed on skis to learn how to take the tight turns needed for mogul fields and other challenges encountered on expert ski runs. Similarly, risks need to be taken on the journey from intermediate to advanced meeting design.

To become an advanced skier or an advanced meeting planner, you need to start as a beginner and progress to intermediate and advanced levels by committing to continuous improvement and taking calculated risks. Many skiers get the help needed to improve their skiing ability from qualified ski instructors who watch them in action and help them improve their skiing skills. Ski instruction gets translated into a higher level of skiing when the skier puts time in on the slopes to practice over and over again until they master what they learned in their ski lessons. Meeting designers can take facilitation training and join a professional society to improve their skills.[10] Meeting designers need to put new skills to use to improve their ability over time. Intermediate meeting design takes the interest and commitment to learn from facilitation experts and apply learnings with enough repetition to excel in meeting design. But advanced meeting design, like advanced skiing, takes enough skill and confidence to take the calculated risks needed for mastery.

There are rewards for those who choose to master a skill. As an expert skier, I get to enjoy some of the most scenic places in the world while getting exercise and having a lot of fun turning through the snow at high speed. As a master meeting designer,[11] I help executives move with intention and efficiency on strategic priorities to decrease risk, increase revenue, improve reputation, and maximize cost savings. In both cases, skiing and meeting design, I have a system to help me perform at my best. Here I share my system for meeting design to help others on their journey to advanced meeting design.

The first step in my system for mastering meeting design is to categorize the meeting in one of four quadrants represented by the following facilitation matrix. I developed this matrix as a tool to avoid repeating a regretful facilitation experience I had as a beginner facilitator. I had just returned from a three-day intensive facilitation workshop at the Creative Problem Solving Group in Buffalo. My boss asked me to facilitate the company's executive leadership team to kick off a new program called Competitiveness Transformation. I used everything I had learned in my training to prepare for this meeting, and I was ready to make a killing! Everything was going according to my plan until the afternoon when the CEO took over the meeting—so much for my killing as a facilitator! Fortunately, I was able to swallow my pride and step aside. But, after the meeting, I needed some serious therapy, so I called one of my facilitation trainers to fix me. He made me feel better by pointing out that the morning session produced the good idea that the CEO was energized to pursue in the afternoon. Yet I still felt like a facilitation failure because we did not stick to my plan. On further reflection, I learned that my meeting design had been focused on improvement for a topic while the CEO was focused on improvement for an outcome. If I had focused on improvement for an outcome rather than improvement for a topic in the meeting design, then the CEO would not have had to change the meeting process on-the-fly.

The facilitation matrix helps a meeting designer target an appropriate type of meeting design. This matrix breaks down the type of challenge that needs to be tackled in a meeting. A team challenge requires doing something differently or doing something better—the vertical axis. The driver of the team challenge is either a topic or an outcome—the horizontal axis. Doing something differently means creating something new, whereas doing things better means improving on something that already exists. A topic is a different kind of driver than an outcome for a team challenge. Consensus on which quadrant the team challenge falls into will help focus the meeting design in the right way for needed outcomes.

DOING THINGS DIFFERENTLY

Develop the possibilities to change from the "as is" state for the topic to a new state	Determine how to change to produce the desired outcome
Explore how to improve the "as is" state for the topic to a better state	Determine how to improve to produce the desired outcome

TOPIC FOCUS — OUTCOME FOCUS

DOING THINGS BETTER

Facilitation Matrix

The upper-right quadrant in the facilitation matrix is for doing things differently with an outcome focus, which is a meeting about an outcome-focused improvement. An example of an outcome-focused improvement is increasing the percentage of women in organizational leadership positions. The outcome is to increase the percentage of women, and the improvement is to address key barriers that limit female participation in organizational leadership positions.

The upper-left quadrant is for doing things differently with a topic focus, which is a meeting about a topic-focused improvement. An example of a such an improvement is a research consortium kick-off meeting for the different players in the energy-retrofit market, such as owners, operators, occupants, architects, building engineers, building consultants, suppliers to the retrofit market, the retrofit workforce, and trainers of the retrofit workforce. The topic for this meeting is the experiences of the different players in the energy retrofit market. The improvement is to improve the experience of the players during a building energy retrofit.

The lower-right quadrant is for doing things better with an outcome focus, which is a meeting for an outcome-focused change. An example of such a change is strategic planning. The outcome for strategic planning is a new performance expectation for a group. The change is for a group to do existing things in a new way and to do new things to be able to achieve the new performance expectation.

Finally, the lower-left quadrant is for doing things better with a topic focus, which is a meeting about a topic-focused change. An example of such a change is a new product identification session with a customer. I did several of these when I was head of an organization's Creative Center. The topic for a new product identification session with a customer is new product opportunities from the intersection of trends with supplier technical capabilities and customer marketing know-how. The change is to uncover attractive new product opportunities for joint development by the supplier and customer and to explore new business models and product offerings by both companies.

The second step in my system for mastering meeting design is defining the meeting purpose, objectives, and outcomes. Strategic and critical thinking are required to uncover and articulate these elements because these are the most abstract elements of meeting design. Meeting purpose is the "why" for the meeting and must make the cost associated with people preparing for and participating in the meeting worthwhile. I use the following format to articulate a meeting purpose: To [topic or outcome], in order to [what the group needs to improve or change], so that [what the group's work will enable the organization to do after the meeting]. Next, the objectives explain the role of participants with respect to the purpose. For example, the objectives clarify how the unique perspectives and expertise of participants will be used in the meeting. Finally, the outcomes are the return on investment of time from participants.

Meeting Purpose:

To gain technical understanding of the most pressing unmet needs associated with the environment in order to brainstorm technical innovations to address the needs so that the organization can leverage its existing and future technical capabilities to address the most impactful challenges.

Meeting Objectives:

- Gain an understanding of how unmet environmental needs might translate into business opportunities for the company.
- Examine how environmental needs may affect the company's businesses.
- Begin to explore how our company's existing and future technical capabilities can address impactful unmet environmental needs.
- Begin the process of identifying partners and resources, such as
  - Government agencies and laboratories to stay abreast of sustainability needs and technical developments;
  - Nongovernmental organizations to monitor public concerns;
  - University professors and laboratories for state-of-the-art technical programs for sustainability;
  - Consultants or advisors that can help our company develop a sustainability strategy.

Meeting Outcomes:

- Generate a comprehensive list of needs and opportunities related to the topic of sustainability for each of nine strategic sustainability themes.
- Identify the top sustainability needs and opportunities for each of the organization's three business areas.
- Prioritize the top sustainability needs and opportunities by business area.
- Develop rationale to address a top need or opportunity for each of the organization's three business areas.

The outcomes are the results that will be delivered from the design. The example on the previous page illustrates a meeting purpose, outcomes, and deliverables.

The third step of my system for mastering meeting design is comprehensive inquiry. I use standard questions to make sure I haven't missed any important information. You can ask these questions of yourself if you happen to be playing the role of both meeting designer and team leader. Alternatively, the designer asks the leader these questions. The questions can be categorized as people, outcome, and process assessments. People assessment questions for meeting design help leverage human resources as follows:

- Who is the highest-level person in the hierarchy who would support the meeting outcomes, and can you get them to weigh in to team meeting design? The higher the level of a meeting sponsor, the higher the motivation of participants.
- Do you have the right people and mix of people on the team in terms of knowledge, expertise, and perspectives to best achieve meeting outcomes? The higher the quality of knowledge, expertise, and perspectives from meeting participants, the higher the quality of meeting outcomes. You can get creative in terms of ways to access knowledge, expertise, and perspectives beyond current team membership.

Outcome assessment questions in meeting design help explore a range of possibilities as follows:

- Imagine the meeting has happened and you are very pleased with what happened. What does that success look like, feel like, and enable to happen? This question helps the team leader and meeting sponsor articulate all aspects of meeting outcomes to maximize impact and increase benefits relative to costs.
- What are the most and least important things to address in this team meeting? This question helps the team leader and

meeting sponsor focus on what really matters, and focus is a way to increase creativity.

- How realistic are expectations of what to accomplish in this team meeting? We all suffer from planning fallacy, which is a nonconscious bias that causes us to underestimate the time and resources it takes to complete a project or task. This question helps the team leader and meeting sponsor and meeting designer eliminate the natural inclination toward planning fallacy as long as the designer seeks specific evidence to back up time estimates for different meeting activities.

Process assessment questions in meeting design help anticipate ways to best support the meeting process as follows:

- What has been tried before to achieve these meeting outcomes, and what happened? This question is as much for the meeting designer as it is for the team leader to assess process options to consider or avoid. This question may also point to content needed to support the meeting outcomes.
- What content is needed for context to level-set meeting participants? With this question, the meeting designer explores the base level of context that all participants need to be able to provide the most constructive input toward the meeting outcomes.

The final step for mastering meeting design is the creative process of integrating the information gathered into a design that is engaging, interactive, and capable of delivering the outcomes. I use the rule of thumb to dedicate at least half of the meeting time to interaction, which means content presentations and instructions take up less than half of the total time. This step can cause changes in other parts of the design, such as revising the meeting purpose, objectives, and outcomes. Meeting design can be messy and iterative, so change is to be expected as the design progresses. I find it helpful to look for sources of inspiration, such as processes and designs that others have used for similar meeting purposes. Input from another meeting designer is also valuable and can be thought-provoking.

Meeting design is optimized by the process used for the design. The process improves with development of facilitation skills and experience designing meetings.

This chapter provided persuasion tactics for meeting designers to convince others to implement their meeting design ideas. The chapter also provided five principles of good meeting design that beginner- and intermediate-level meeting designers can use for ideas on how to improve their approach to meeting design. Finally, the chapter described the components of meeting design and shared a system for mastering this design. A skillful meeting design can compensate for shortcomings in other areas as a path to achieve meeting outcomes.

Here are some reflection exercises and questions for this chapter on meeting design to enhance learning:

- How might the concepts presented for mastery of meeting design apply to another skill or topic you are interested in mastering? List as many ideas as you can think of and then select the top couple of ideas that you would like to try.

- In what ways might you improve your approach to meeting design for a meeting you are leading? List as many ideas as you can think of and choose the top one you would like to implement for your next meeting.

- What insights did you have about meeting design?

ENDNOTES

INTRODUCTION

1. Behfnam Tabrizi. "75% of Teams Are Dysfunctional." *Harvard Business Review*. June 23, 2015. *https://hbr.org*.

2. Elizabeth G. Hunter and Graham D. Rowles. "Leaving a Legacy: Toward a Typology." *Journal of Aging Studies* 19 (2005): 327–47.

3. Department of University Marketing. "Penn State Up Close." 2015. *PennState. https://admissions.psu.edu*.

4. *Build Your Trust Advantage: Leadership in the Era of Data and AI Everywhere*, 20th ed., IBM Institute for Business Value (November 2019): 31. *https://www.ibm.com*.

5. Dietrich Dörner and Joachim Funke. "Complex Problem Solving: What It Is and What It Is Not." *Frontiers in Psychology* 8 (July 11, 2017): Article 1153, 1–11.

6. Anita Williams Woolley, Ishani Aggarwal, and Thomas W. Malone. "Collective Intelligence and Group Performance." *Current Directions in Psychological Science* 24:6 (2015): 420–24.

7. Heidi A. Wayment, Jack J. Bauer, and Kateryna Sylaska. "The Quiet Ego Scale: Measuring the Compassionate Self-Identity." *Journal of Happiness Studies* 15:3 (July 5, 2014): 999–1033.

8. Keith Sawyer. *Zig Zag: The Surprising Path to Greater Creativity* (San Francisco: Jossey-Bass, 2013), 53–56.

9. Woolley, Aggarwal, and Malone. "Collective Intelligence and Group Performance." 420–24.

CHAPTER 1

1. Kendra Cherry. "Gardner's Theory of Multiple Intelligences." *Very Well Mind*. July 17, 2019. *https://www.verywellmind.com*.

2. John F. Kihlstrom and Nancy Cantor. "Social Intelligence." In *Handbook of Intelligence,* 2nd ed., ed. R. J. Sternberg (Cambridge, UK: Cambridge University Press, 2000), 359–79 (an update appeared in the 3rd edition, 2011). *https://www.ocf.berkeley.edu.*

3. Susanne Weise and Heinz-Martin Suss. "Social Intelligence—A Review and Critical Discussion of Measurement Concepts." *An International Handbook of Emotional Intelligence.* (January 2005): 203-30. *https://www.researchgate.net.*

4. Steve Mithen. "Mind, Brain, and Material Culture: An Archeological Perspective." In *Evolution and the Human Mind: Modularity, Language, and Meta-Cognition,* ed. Peter Caruthers and Andrew Chamberlain (Cambridge, UK: Cambridge University Press, 2000), 207.

5. Matt Salter. "Homeostasis Examples." *Your Dictionary.* *https://examples.yourdictionary.com.*

6. Matthew Lieberman. "The Social Brain and Its Superpowers." October 7, 2013. *TEDx Talk. https://www.youtube.com.*

7. Matthew D. Lieberman. "Are We Wired to Be Social?" *Psychology Today.* October 23, 2013. *https://www.psychologytoday.com.*

8. Matthew Pantell, David Rehkopf, Douglas Jutte, S. Leonard Syme, John Balmes, and Nancy Adler. "Social Isolation: A Predictor of Mortality Comparable to Traditional Clinical Risk Factors." *American Journal of Public Health* 103:11 (November 2013): 2056–62.

9. George C. Fraser. *Click: Ten Truths for Building Extraordinary Relationships* (New York: McGraw-Hill, 2008), 178.

10. Sheldon Cohen. "Social Relationships and Health." *American Psychologist* 59:8 (November 2004): 676–84.

11. Robin I. M. Dunbar. "The Social Brain Hypothesis." *Evolutionary Anthropology* 6:5 (1998): 178–90.

12. Daniel Goleman. *Social Intelligence: The New Science of Social Relationships* (New York: Bantam Books, 2006), 277.

13. "How to Strengthen Social Relationships." *Real Warriors.* October 26, 2020. *http://www.realwarriors.net.*

14. Christina Gough. "Health Club Industry: Worldwide Revenue by Region." *Statista.* October 29, 2020. *https://www.statista.com.*

15. Laura Wood. "The $72 Billion Weight Loss and Diet Control Market in the United States, 2019–2023: Why Meal Replacements Are

Still Booming, but Not OTC Diet Pills." *ResearchAndMarkets*. February 25, 2019. *https://apnews.com*.

16. A. Oloruntoba. "Revenue of the Apparel Market Worldwide by Country 2019." *Statista*. August 26, 2020. *https://www.statista.com*.

17. Mathew G. Wilson, Georgina M. Ellison, and N. Tim Cable. "Basic Science Behind the Cardiovascular Benefits of Exercise." *British Journal of Sports Medicine* 50 (2016): 93–99.

18. J. W. R. Twisk, B. J. Staal, M. N. Brinkman, H. C. G. Kemper, and W. van Mechelen. "Tracking of Lung Function Parameters and the Longitudinal Relationship with Lifestyle." *European Respiratory Journal* 12 (1998): 627–34.

19. John Medina. *Brain Rules: 12 Principles for Surviving and Thriving at Work, Home, and School* (Seattle, WA: Pear Press, 2014), 19–35.

20. Peter Salmon. "Effects of Physical Exercise on Anxiety, Depression and Sensitivity to Stress: A Unifying Theory." *Clinical Psychology Review* 21:1 (February 2001): 33–61.

21. Elisa A. Marques, Jorge Mota, Leondro Machado, Filipa Sousa, Margarida Coelho, Pedro Moreia, and Joana Carvalho. "Multicomponent Training Program with Weight-Bearing Exercises Elicits Favorable Bone Density, Muscle Strength and Balance Adaptations in Older Women." *Calcified Tissue International* 88 (2011): 117–29.

22. Juan C. Aristizabal, Daniel Freidenreich, Britannie Volk, Brian Kupchak, Catherine Saenz, Carl M. Maresh, William J. Kraemer, and J. S. Volek. "Effect of Resistance Training on Resting Metabolic Rate and Its Estimation by a Dual-Energy X-ray Absorptiometry Metabolic Map." *European Journal of Clinical Nutrition* 69 (2015): 831–36.

23. Richard Weil. "Aerobic Exercise." *Emedicine Health*. March 5, 2020. *http://www.emedicinehealth.com*.

24. David Dubail. "Exercise and Fitness Tips: How to Monitor Heart Rate During Exercise." March 29, 2010. *https://www.youtube.com*.

25. Tim Newman. "All You Need to Know About Shin Splints." *Medical News Today*. October 13, 2017. *http://www.medicalnewstoday.com*.

26. Gina R. Poe, Christine M. Walsh, and Theresa E. Bjorness. "Cognitive Neuroscience of Sleep." *Progress in Brain Research* 185 (2010): 1–19.

27. Jeffrey J. Iliff, Minghuan Wang, Yonghong Liao, Benjamin A. Plogg, Weiguo Peng, Georg A. Gundersen, Helene Benveniste, G.

Edward Vates, Rashid Deane, Steven A. Goldman, Erlend A. Nagelhus, and Maiken Nedergaard. "A Paravascular Pathway Facilitates CSF Flow Through the Brain Parenchyma and the Clearance of Interstitial Solutes, Including Amyloid Beta." *Science Translational Medicine* 4:147 (2012): 147ra111.

28. Lulu Xie, Hongyi Kang, Qiwu Xu, Michael J. Chen, Yonghong Liao, Meenakshisundaram Thiyagarajan, John O'Donnell, Daniel J. Christensen, Charles Nicholson, Jeffrey J. Iliff, Takahiro Takano, Rashid Deane, and Maiken Nedergaard. "Sleep Drives Metabolic Clearance from the Adult Brain." *Science* 342 (October 18, 2013): 373–77.

29. Max Hirshkowitz, Kaitlyn Whiton, Steven M. Albert, Cathy Alessi, Oliviero Bruni, Lydia DonCarlos, Nancy Hazen, John Herman, Eliot S. Katz, Leila Kheirandish-Gozal, David N. Neubauer, Anne E. O'Donnell, Maurice Ohayon, John Peever, Robert Rawding, Ramesh C. Sachdeva, Belinda Setters, Michael V. Vitiello, J. Catesby Ware, Paula J. Adams Hillard, M. Hirshkowitz et al. "National Sleep Foundation's Sleep Time Duration Recommendations: Methodology and Results Summary." *Sleep Health* 1:1 (2015): 40–43.

30. "Five Clusters of Sleep Patterns." *National Sleep Foundation.* *https://sleepfoundation.org.*

31. Maurice Ohayon, Emerson M. Wickwire, Max Hirshkowitz, Steven M. Albert, Alon Avidan, Frank J. Daly, Yves Dauvilliers, Raffaele Ferri, Constance Fung, David Gozal, Nancy Hazen, Andrew Krystal, Kenneth Lichstein, Monica Mallampalli, Giuseppe Plazzi, Robert Rawding, Frank A. Scheer, Virend Somers, and Michael V. Vitiello. "National Sleep Foundation's Sleep Quality Recommendations: First Report." *Sleep Health* 3:1 (2017): 6–19.

32. Michelle E. Watts, Roger Pocock, and Charles Claudianos. "Brain Energy and Oxygen Metabolism: Emerging Role in Normal Function and Disease." *Frontiers in Molecular Neuroscience* 11:216 (June 22, 2018): 1–13.

33. Christina Feldman and Jack Kornfield, ed. *Stories of the Spirit, Stories of the Heart: Parables of the Spiritual Path from Around the World* (San Francisco: HarperCollins Publishers, 1991).

34. Patty Van Cappellen, Vassilis Saroglou, Caroline Iweins, Maria Piovesana, and Barbara L. Fredrickson. "Self-Transcendent Positive

Emotions Increase Spirituality Through Basic World Assumptions." *Cognition and Emotion* 27:8 (2013): 1378–94.

35. Patty Van Cappellen, Baldwin M. Way, Suzannah F. Isgett, and Barbara L. Fredrickson. "Effects of Oxytocin Administration on Spirituality and Emotional Responses to Meditation." *Social Cognitive and Affective Neuroscience* 11:10 (2016): 1579–87.

36. Frederic Brussat and Mary Ann Brussat. "Spiritual Practice Toolkit." *Spirituality and Practice. https://www.spiritualityandpractice.com.*

37. Nathaniel Elkins-Brown, Rimma Tepper, and Michael Inzlicht. "How Mindfulness Enhances Self Control." *Mindfulness in Social Psychology.* April 2017. *https://www.researchgate.net.*

38. David J. Creswell. "Mindfulness Interventions." *Annual Review of Psychology* 68 (2017): 491–516.

39. Wei Deng, James B. Aimone, and Fred H. Gage. "New Neurons and New Memories: How Does Adult Hippocampal Neurogenesis Affect Learning and Memory?" *Nature Reviews Neuroscience* 11 (May 2010): 339–50.

40. Guo-li Ming and Hongjun Song. "Adult Neurogenesis in the Mammalian Brain: Significant Answers and Significant Questions." *Neuron* 70 (May 2011): 687–702.

41. Steven L. Bressler and Venod Menon. "Large-scale Brain Networks in Cognition: Emerging Methods and Principles." *Trends in Cognitive Sciences* 14 (2010): 277–90.

42. Elizabeth Gould, Anna Beylin, Patima Tanapat, Alison Reeves, and Tracey J. Shors. "Learning Enhances Adult Neurogenesis in the Hippocampal Formation." *Nature Neuroscience* 2:3 (March 1999): 260–65.

43. Andrew R. A. Conway and Sarah J. Getz. "Cognitive Ability: Does Working Memory Training Enhance Intelligence?" *Current Biology* 20:8 (2010): R362–R364.

44. Keith Sawyer. *Zig Zag: The Surprising Path to Greater Creativity* (New York: Jossey-Bass, 2013), 49–72.

45. Scott Barry Kaufman. "The Real Neuroscience of Creativity." *Scientific American.* August 19, 2013. *https://blogs.scientificamerican.com.*

46. Scott Barry Kaufman and Carolyn Gregoire. *Wired to Create: Unraveling the Mysteries of the Creative Mind* (New York: Perigee, 2015), 43.

47. Medina. *Brain Rules.* 19–81 and 201–22.

48. M. J. Dauncey. "Recent Advances in Nutrition, Genes and Brain Health." *Proceedings of the Nutrition Society* 71:4 (2012): 581–91.

49. Tom Kelley and David Kelley. *Creative Confidence: Unleashing the Creative Potential Within Us All* (New York: Crown Business, 2013).

50. Kerry Patterson, Joseph Grenny, Ron McMillan, and Al Switzler. *Crucial Conversations: Tools for Talking When Stakes Are High,* 2nd ed. (New York: McGraw-Hill, 2012), 54.

51. Daisy Grewal and Peter Salovey. "Feeling Smart: The Science of Emotional Intelligence." *American Scientist* 93 (July/August 2005): 330–39.

52. P. J. O'Connor, Andrew Hill, Maria Kaya, and Brett Martin. "The Measurement of Emotional Intelligence: A Critical Review of the Literature and Recommendations for Researchers and Practitioners." *Frontiers in Psychology* 10:1116 (May 2019): 1116.

53. Jaak Panksepp. "The Science of Emotions." January 13, 2014. *https://www.youtube.com.*

54. John Martin in a NeuroLeadership Institute "Train the Trainer" presentation on May 30, 2017.

55. Kathryn Thory. "A Gendered Analysis of Emotional Intelligence in the Workplace: Issues and Concerns for Human Resource Development." *Human Resource Development Review* 12:2 (2012): 221–44.

56. "Pyramid: Women in S&P 500 Companies." *Catalyst.* January 15, 2020. *https://www.catalyst.org.*

CHAPTER 2

1. Dan Pink. "The Puzzle of Motivation." *TED Talks.* July 2009. *https://www.ted.com;* Daniel H. Pink. *Drive: The Surprising Truth About What Motivates Us* (New York: Riverhead Books, 2009).

2. Aaron Hurst. "The Purpose Economy." June 29, 2014. *https://www.youtube.com;* Aaron Hurst. *The Purpose Economy: How Your Desire for Impact, Personal Growth, and Community Is Changing the World* (California: Independently published, 2014).

3. Daniel H. Pink. *A Whole New Mind: Moving from the Information Age to the Conceptual Age* (New York: Riverhead Books, 2005); Chris Laszlo and Judy Sorum Brown. *Flourishing Enterprise: The New Spirit*

of *Business* (Stanford, CA: Stanford University Press, 2014); Frederick Chavalit Tsao and Chris Laszlo. *Quantum Leadership: New Consciousness in Business* (Stanford, CA: Stanford Business Books, 2019); Scott Barry Kaufman. *Transcend: The New Science of Self-Actualization* (New York: Penguin Random House, 2020).

4. Oprah Winfrey. "Oprah's Supersoul Conversations." *http://www.supersoul.tv;* and Oprah's SuperSoul Conversations podcast where you listen to podcasts (Apple Podcasts, Stitcher, Android Podcast apps like Doublepod).

5. Morten T. Hansen. *Great at Work: How Top Performers Do Less, Work Better, and Achieve More* (New York: Simon & Schuster, 2018).

6. Aliya Alimujiang, Ashley Wiensch, Jonathan Boss, Nancy L. Fleischer, Alison M. Mondul, Karen McLean, Bhramar Mukherjee, and Celeste Leigh Pearce. "Association Between Life Purpose and Mortality Among US Adults Older than 50 Years." *JAMA Network Open* 2:5 (2019): e194270. *http://doi.org/10.1001/jamanetworkopen.2019.4270.*

7. Oprah Winfrey and Dan Pink. "Full Episode: Oprah Winfrey and Dan Pink." *Oprah.com. http://www.oprah.com.*

8. Pamela D. McLean and Frederick M. Hudson. *Life Launch: A Passionate Guide to the Rest of Your Life* (Washington, DC: Hudson Institute Press, 1995), 66–73.

9. Robert N. Llewellyn. "The Four Career Concepts." *SHRM.* September 1, 2002. *https://www.shrm.org.*

10. William Bridges. *Creating You & Co.: Learn to Think Like the CEO of Your Own Career* (Cambridge MA: Da Copa Press, 1997), 49–60.

11. Peter M. Senge. *The Fifth Discipline: The Art and Practice of the Learning Organization* (New York: Doubleday/Currency, 1990), 139–73.

12. Hilary Scarlett. "Neuroscience: Helping Employees Through Change." *CEB Blog.* January 21, 2013. *https://www.cebglobal.com.*

13. Merve Emre. "Personality Puzzler: Is There Any Science Behind Myers-Briggs?" *Knowledge@Wharton.* November 8, 2018. *https://knowledge.wharton.upenn.edu.*

14. Scot Wall. "Explore Personality Types to Understand Others, Understand Ourselves." *Chron.* September 8, 2016. *http://www.chron.com.*

15. "MBTI Basics." *The Myers and Briggs Foundation. http://www.myersbriggs.org.*

16. "Free Personality Test." *16Personalities*. *https://www.16personalities.com*.

17. "ENFJ Personality Type." *Truity*. *https://www.truity.com*.

18. Jhoon. "Emotional Triggers of Each MBTI Type." *Astroligion*. *https://astroligion.com*.

19. Jenna Birch. "This Is How You Handle Conflict, According to Your Myers-Briggs Personality Type." *WellAndGood*. September 29, 2018. *https://www.wellandgood.com*.

20. Linda V. Berens, Linda K. Ernst, and Melissa A. Smith. *Quick Guide to the 16 Personality Types: Applying Team Essentials to Create Effective Teams* (New York: Telos Publications, 2004). *http://www.bestfittype.com*.

21. "The Traditional Enneagram." *The Enneagram Institute*. *https://www.enneagraminstitute.com*.

22. "Emotional Intelligence Is the True Stuff of Success." *Essi Systems*. *https://essisystems.com*.

23. Veronika Huta. "An Overview of Hedonic and Eudaimonic Well-Being Concepts." *Handbook of Media Use and Well-Being*. November 11, 2015. Chapter 2. *https://www.researchgate.net*.

24. Thea Buckley. "What Happens to the Brain During Cognitive Dissonance?" *Scientific American*. November 1, 2015. *https://www.scientificamerican.com*.

25. "The Science of Stress." *National Geographic*. August 19, 2013. *https://www.youtube.com*.

26. Amanda Blanck, managing partner at Deviate, runs group coaching sessions. *Deviate*. *http://www.offtrackonpurpose.com*.

27. W. R. Miller, J. C'de Baca, D. B. Matthews, and P. L. Wilbourne, "2001 Personal Values Card Sort." *University of New Mexico*. *http://www.motivationalinterviewing.org*.

28. Madhuleena Roy Chowdhury. "The 3 Best Questionnaires for Measuring Values." *Positive Psychology*. January 9, 2020. *https://positivepsychology.com*.

29. Martin E. P. Seligman, Tracey A. Steen, and Christopher Peterson. "Positive Psychology Progress: Empirical Validation of Interventions." *American Psychologist* 60:5 (July–August 2005): 410–21.

30. Donna Fisher and Sandy Vilas. *Power Networking: 59 Secrets for Personal and Professional Success* (New York: Bard Press, 1992), 52–55.

31. "The MAPP™ Career Assessment Test." *MAPP. https://www .assessment.com.*

32. Dawna Markova and Angie McArthur. *Collaborative Intelligence: Thinking with People Who Think Differently* (New York: Random House, 2015), 107–68, Valerie Patrick and Dawna Markova. "A Neuroscientific Approach to Improving Collaboration." *Fulcrum Connection LLC.* May 4, 2016. *https://fulcrumconnection.com;* Valerie Patrick and Angie McArthur. "How Inquiry Improves Collaboration." *Fulcrum Connection LLC.* June 22, 2016. *https://fulcrumconnection.com.*

33. Laura Morgan Roberts, Gretchen Spreitzer, Jane E. Dutton, Robert E. Quinn, Emily D. Heaphy, and Brianna Barker. "How to Play to Your Strengths." *Harvard Business Review.* January 2005. *https://hbr.org.*

34. "MindManager: Powerful Visualization Tools and Mindmapping Software." *Mindjet. https://www.mindjet.com.*

35. Anita Williams Woolley, Ishani Aggarwal, and Thomas W. Malone. "Collective Intelligence and Group Performance." *Current Directions in Psychological Science* 24:6 (2015): 420–24.

36. Peter Sherzer, Edith Leveille, Andre Achim, Emilie Boisseau, and Emmanuel Stip. "A Study of Theory of Mind in Paranoid Schizophrenia: A Theory of Many Theories?" *Frontiers in Psychology* 3:432 (November 2012). *http://doi.org/10.3389/fpsyg.2012.00432.*

37. Lucy Anne Livingston, Bethany Carr, and Punit Shah. "Recent Advances and New Directions in Measuring Theory of Mind in Autistic Adults." *Journal of Autism and Developmental Disorders* 49 (2019): 1738–44.

38. Caitlin E. V. Mahy, Louis J. Moses, and Jennifer H. Pfeifer. "How and Where: Theory-of-Mind in the Brain." *Developmental Cognitive Neuroscience* 9 (2014): 68–81.

39. Elena Cavallini, Frederica Bianco, Sara Bottiroli, Alessia Rossi, Tomaso Vecchi, and Serena Lecce. "Training for Generalization in Theory of Mind: A Study with Older Adults." *Frontiers in Psychology* 6:1123 (August 2015). *https://doi.org/10.3389/fpsyg.2015.01123.*

CHAPTER 3

1. Angela Duckworth. *Grit: The Power of Passion and Perseverance* (New York: Scribner, 2016).

2. Aaqib Saeed, Stojan Trajanovski, Maurice Van Keulen, and Jan Erp. "Deep Physiological Arousal Detection in a Driving Simulator Using Wearable Sensors." IEEE ICDM Conference Paper. November 18, 2017. *https://www.researchgate.net/.*

3. Foundations in NeuroLeadership Certification Program by NeuroLeadership Institute in Spring 2018.

4. Daniel Goleman. *Social Intelligence: The Revolutionary New Science of Human Relationships* (New York: Bantam Books, 2006).

5. Carol S. Dweck. *Mindset: The New Psychology of Success* (New York: Random House, 2016).

6. "6 Keys to Having It All" workshop by Joe Folkman at the Annual Association for Talent Development meeting, June 11, 2018.

7. Morten T. Hansen. *Great at Work: How Top Performers Do Less, Work Better, and Achieve More* (New York: Simon & Schuster, 2018).

8. Adapted from Michael Wilkinson. *The Executive Guide to Facilitating Strategy* (Atlanta, GA: Leadership Strategies Publishing, 2011).

9. Elliot T. Berkman and Matthew D. Lieberman. "Approaching the Bad and Avoiding the Good: Lateral Prefrontal Cortical Asymmetry Distinguishes Between Action and Valence." *Journal of Cognitive Neuroscience* 22:9 (2010): 1970–79; and Jeffrey A. Gray. "The Psychophysiological Basis of Introversion-Extraversion." *Behavior Research and Therapy* 8:3 (1970): 249–66.

10. Anita Woolley. "Can Collective Intelligence Be Measured and Predicted?" *Carnegie Mellon University Tepper School of Business.* *https://www.cmu.edu.*

11. Amy Edmondson. "How to Turn a Group of Strangers into a Team." *TED Talks.* October 2017. *https://www.ted.com.*

12. Paul J. Zak. "The Neuroscience of Trust." *Harvard Business Review.* January–February 2017. *https://hbr.org.*

13. Antoine Besnard, Yuan Gao, Michael TaeWoo Kim, Hannah Twarkowski, Alexander Keith Reed, Tomer Langberg, Wendy Feng, Xiangmin Xu, Dieter Saur, Larry S. Zweifel, Ian Davison, and Amar Sahay. "Dorsolateral Septum Somatostatin Interneurons Gate Mobility to Calibrate Context Specific Behavioral Fear Responses." *Nature Neuroscience* 22:3 (March 2019): 436–46. doi:10.1038/s41593-018-0330-y.

14. David Rock. "Managing with the Brain in Mind." *Strategy + Business*. August 27, 2009. *https://www.strategy-business.com*.

15. Carol S. Dweck. *Mindset: The New Psychology of Success* (New York: Random House, 2016).

16. Mario Livio. "The 'Why' Behind Asking Why: The Science of Curiosity." *Knowledge@Wharton*. August 23, 2017. *https://knowledge.wharton.upenn.edu*.

17. Amy Edmondson. "How to Turn a Group of Strangers into a Team." *TED Talks*. October 2017. *https://www.ted.com*.

18. Matthew D. Lieberman. *Social: Why Our Brains Are Wired to Connect* (New York: Crown Publishers, 2013).

19. Valerie Patrick and Vanessa Druskat. "How to Increase the Emotional Intelligence of a Team." *Fulcrum Connection LLC*. April 21, 2017. *https://fulcrumconnection.com*.

20. Jacob Israelashvili, Suzanne Oosterwijk, Disa Sauter, and Agneta Fischer. "Knowing Me, Knowing You: Emotion Differentiation in Oneself Is Associated with Recognition of Others' Emotions." *Cognition and Emotion* 33:7 (2019): 1461–71.

21. "Name It to Tame It." *Power of TED*. July 21, 2017. *https://powerofted.com*.

22. Scott G. Isaksen and Goran Ekvall. "Development of the Situational Outlook Questionnaire: A Technical Resource." (2nd edition by the Creative Problem Solving Group). *https://www.soqonline.net*.

23. Arne Dietrich. *How Creativity Happens in the Brain* (London: Palgrave MacMillan, 2015).

24. W. R. Miller, J. C'de Baca, D. B. Matthews, and P. L. Wilbourne. "Personal Values Card Sort." *University of New Mexico*. 2001. *http://www.motivationalinterviewing.org*.

CHAPTER 4

1. Jay J. Van Bhavel, Leor M. Hackel, and Y. Jenny Xiao. "The Group Mind: The Pervasive Influence of Social Identity on Cognition." *Research and Perspectives in Neurosciences* 21:1 (2014): 41–56.

2. Anita Williams Woolley, Ishani Aggarwal, and Thomas W. Malone. "Collective Intelligence and Group Performance." *Current Directions in Psychological Science* 24:6 (2015): 420–24.

3. Don A. Moore and George Loewenstein. "Self-Interest, Automaticity, and the Psychology of Conflict of Interest." *Social Justice Research* 17:2 (June 2004): 189–202.

4. P. Hart. "Irving L. Janis' Victims of Groupthink," *Political Psychology* 12:2 (June 1991): 247–78.

5. Stephen R. Covey. *Living the 7 Habits: Stories of Courage and Inspiration* (New York: Simon & Schuster, 2000), 304.

6. Ute R. Hülsheger, Neil Anderson, and Jesus F. Salgado. "Team-level Predictors of Innovation at Work: A Comprehensive Meta-Analysis Spanning Three Decades of Research." *Journal of Applied Psychology* 94:5 (2009): 1128–45.

7. 2015 Coursera Course by Dr. Scott DeRue, University of Michigan.

8. J. Richard Hackman and Neil Vidmar. "Effects of Size and Task Type on Group Performance and Member Reactions." *Sociometry* 33:1 (1970): 37–54.

9. Rich Karlgaard and Michael S. Malone. *Team Genius: The New Science of High-Performing Organizations* (New York: HarperCollins Publishers, 2015).

10. David Rock. *Your Brain at Work: Strategies for Overcoming Distraction, Regaining Focus, and Working Smarter All Day Long* (New York: HarperCollins Publishers, 2009).

11. International Association of Facilitators. "Find an IAF Certified Professional Facilitator." *International Association of Facilitators.* *https://www.iaf-world.org.*

12. Keith Sawyer. *Group Genius: The Creative Power of Collaboration* (New York: Basic Books, 2007).

13. Joseph Grenny, Ron McMillan, and Al Switzler. *Crucial Conversations: Tools for Talking When Stakes Are High.* (New York: McGraw-Hill, 2012), 58.

14. Emily Teding van Berkhout and John M. Malouff. "The Efficacy of Empathy Training: A Meta-analysis of Randomized Control Trials." *Journal of Counseling Psychology* 63:1 (2015): 32–41.

15. Kelise K. Stewart, James E. Carr, and Linda A. LeBlanc. "Evaluation of Family-Implemented Behavioral Skills Training for Teaching Social Skills to a Child with Asperger's Disorder." *Clinical Case Studies* 6:3 (June 2007): 252–62.

16. "Project Implicit." *Harvard University.* *https://implicit.harvard.edu.*

17. David Gelles. "Julie Sweet of Accenture Could See Her Future. So She Quit Her Job." *New York Times*. January 2, 2019. *https://www .nytimes.com*.

18. Mina Cikara and Jay J. Van Bhavel. "The Neuroscience of Intergroup Relations: An Integrative Review." *Perspectives on Psychological Science* 9 (2014): 245–74.

19. Thandie Newton. "Embracing Otherness, Embracing Myself." *TED Talks*. July 2011. *https://www.ted.com*.

20. David Rock and Christine Cox. "SCARF in 2012: Updating the Social Neuroscience of Collaborating with Others." *NeuroLeadership Journal* 4 (2012): 1–14.

21. Matthew D. Lieberman, David Rock, Heidi Grant Halvorson, and Christine Cox. "Breaking Bias Updated: The SEEDS Model." *NeuroLeadership Journal* 6 (November 2015): 1–18.

22. Barbara L. Fredrickson and Marcial F. Losada. "Positive Affect and the Complex Dynamics of Human Flourishing." *American Psychologist* 60:7 (October 2005): 678–86.

23. Christine Cox, Josh Davis, David Rock, Camille Inge, Heide Grant, Kamila Sip, Jacqui Grey, and Lisa Rock. "The Science of Inclusion: How We Can Leverage the Brain to Build Smarter Teams." *NeuroLeadership Journal* 6 (November 2016): 1–17.

24. "What Is the ADKAR Model?" *Prosci. https://www.prosci.com;* Jeffrey M. Hiatt, *ADKAR* (Loveland: Prosci Learning Center Publications, 2006).

25. "8-Step Process for Leading Change." *Kotter Inc. https://www .kotterinc.com*.

26. "The Macroscope Methodology Framework." *Macroscope Community. https://macroscope.ca.fujitsu.com*.

27. John H. Zenger and Joseph R. Folkman. *The Extraordinary Leader: Turning Good Managers into Great Leaders* (New York: McGraw-Hill, 2009).

28. Roy Maurer. "New Employee Onboarding Guide." *SHRM. https://www.shrm.org*.

CHAPTER 5

1. Anita Williams Woolley, Ishani Aggarwal, and Thomas W. Malone. "Collective Intelligence and Group Performance." *Current Directions in Psychological Science* 24:6 (2015): 420–24.

2. Scott G. Isaksen and Goran Ekvall. "Conceptual and Historical Foundations of the Situational Outlook Questionnaire: A Technical Resource for the SOQ," 2nd ed. (Creative Problem Solving Group, Inc., 2015), 65. *https://soqonline.azurewebsites.net.*

3. Laurie R. Weingart, Kristin Behfar, Corinne Bendersky, Gergana Todorova, and Karen A. Jehn. "The Directness and Oppositional Intensity of Conflict Expression." *Academy of Management Review* 40:2 (April 2014). *http://doi.org/10.5465/amr.2013.0124.*

4. Daniel Kahneman. *Thinking Fast and Slow* (New York: Farrar, Straus and Giroux, 2011).

5. Keith Sawyer. *Zig Zag: The Surprising Path to Greater Creativity* (New York: Jossey-Bass, 2013).

6. Isaksen and Ekvall. "Conceptual and Historical Foundations of the Situational Outlook Questionnaire."

7. Teresa Amabile and Steve Kramer. *The Progress Principle: Using Small Wins to Ignite Joy, Engagement, and Creativity at Work* (Brighton, MA: Harvard Business Review Press, 2011).

8. Christian Byrge and Soren Hansen. "The Creative Platform: A New Paradigm for Teaching Creativity." *Problems of Education in the 21st Century* 18 (2009): 33–50.

9. Scott Barry Kaufman and Carolyn Gregoire. *Wired to Create: Unraveling the Mysteries of the Creative Mind* (New York: Perigree, 2015).

10. Kaufman and Gregoire. *Wired to Create.*

11. Bob Sutton. "Three Unmistakable Signs You're in a Toxic Workplace." *INC. magazine.* September 19, 2017. *https://www.inc.com.*

12. Creative Problem Solving Group. "What Is Climate?" *Situational Outlook Questionnaire. https://www.soqonline.net.*

13. Christian Byrge and Soren Hansen. *The Creative Platform: A Handbook for Creative Processes in Education and Worklife* (Denmark: Aarlborg University, 2015).

14. Edoardo Binda Zane. "9 Unique Teambuilding Games for Meetings That Work." *http://www.edoardo-binda-zane.com.*

15. Dawna Markova and Angie McArthur. *Collaborative Intelligence: Thinking with People Who Think Differently* (New York: Random House, 2015).

16. Certification in the Foundations of NeuroLeadership program by the NeuroLeadership Institute in the Fall of 2017.

17. Keith Sawyer. "The Cognitive Neuroscience of Creativity: A Critical Review." *Creativity Research Journal* 23:2 (2011): 137–54.

18. Sawyer. *Zig Zag.*

19. Keith Sawyer. *Group Genius: The Creative Power of Collaboration* (New York: Basic Books, 2007).

20. Mark Jung-Beeman, Azurii Collier, and John Kounios. "How Insight Happens: Learning from the Brain." *NeuroLeadership Journal* 1 (2008): 1–6.

21. Catherine Clifford. "Salesforce CEO Marc Benioff: Why We Have 'Mindfulness Zones' Where Employees Put Away Phones, Clear Their Minds." *CNBC.* November 5, 2019. *https://www.cnbc.com.*

22. Stefan Wuchty, Benjamin Jones, and Brian Uzzi. "The Increasing Dominance of Teams in Production of Knowledge." *Science* 316:5827 (2007): 1036–39.

23. Amy C. Edmondson. "Teamwork on the Fly: How to Master the Art of Teaming." *Harvard Business Review* (April 2012): 72–80.

24. Adapted from "5 Shades of Power: The Organizational Taboo" workshop presented by Dr. Drea Zigarmi and Dr. Taylor Peyton Roberts at the Annual Association for Talent Development meeting on May 8, 2018.

25. Stephen M. R. Covey with Rebecca R. Merrill. *The Speed of Trust: The One Thing That Changes Everything* (New York: Free Press, 2018).

26. Andrew J. Elliot and Marcy A. Church. "A Hierarchical Model of Approach and Avoidance Achievement Motivation." *Journal of Personality and Social Psychology* 72:1 (1997): 218–32.

27. David Rock. *Your Brain at Work: Strategies for Overcoming Distraction, Regaining Focus, and Working Smarter All Day Long* (New York: HarperCollins Publishers, 2009).

28. Elliot T. Berkman and David Rock. "AIM: An Integrative Model of Goal Pursuit." *Neuroleadership Journal* 5 (September 2014): 1–15.

CHAPTER 6

1. Anita Williams Woolley, Ishani Aggarwal, and Thomas W. Malone. "Collective Intelligence and Group Performance." *Current Directions in Psychological Science* 24:6 (2015): 420–24.

2. "IAF Core Competencies." *International Association of Facilitators.* *https://www.iaf-world.org.*

3. Valerie Patrick and Bill Shephard. "How Facilitation Helps Groups Innovate and Change." *Fulcrum Connection LLC.* December 8, 2015. *https://fulcrumconnection.com.*

4. Scott Isakesen and Bill Shephard. "Igniting Creative Potential: A Focus on Facilitation." *Creative Problem Solving Group.* *https://www.cpsb .com.*

5. Scott Isaksen. "Facilitating Creative Problem-Solving Groups." *Psychology.* 1992. *https://pdfs.semanticscholar.org.*

6. Woolley, Aggarwal, and Malone. "Collective Intelligence and Group Performance." 420–424.

7. "IT Governance Charter Toolkit." *Advisory Board.* October 12, 2018. *https://www.advisory.com.*

8. "Find an IAF Certified Professional Facilitator." *International Association of Facilitators.* *https://www.iaf-world.org.*

9. Neuroscientist Dr. Christine Cox in Certificate in the Foundations of NeuroLeadership Program, Week 2, November 2017.

10. Cyrus K. Foroughi, Nicole E. Werner, Erik T. Nelson, and Deborah A. Boehm-Davis. "Do Interruptions Affect Quality of Work?" *Human Factors: The Journal of the Human Factors and Ergonomics Society* 56:7 (2014): 1262–71.

11. Eyal Ophir, Clifford Nass, and Anthony D. Wagner. "Cognitive Control in Media Multitaskers." *Proceedings of the National Academy of Sciences* 106:37 (September 15, 2009): 15583–87.

12. Tony Ro, Charlotte Russel, and Nilli Lavie. "Changing Faces: A Detection Advantage in the Flicker Paradigm." *Psychological Science* 12:1 (January 2001): 94–99.

13. Leda Cosmides and John Tooby. "Evolutionary Psychology: New Perspectives on Cognition and Motivation." *Annual Review of Psychology* 64:1 (2013): 201–29.

14. Roser Canigueral and Antonia F. de C. Hamilton. "The Role of Eye Gaze During Natural Social Interactions in Typical and Autistic People." *Frontiers in Psychology* 10:560 (March 2019). *https://doi .org/10.3389/fpsyg.2019.00560.*

15. Adam K. Anderson, Peter E. Wais, and John D. E. Gabrieli. "Emotion Enhances Remembrance of Neutral Events Past." *Proceedings of the National Academy of Sciences* 103:5 (January 31, 2006): 1599–1604.

16. Foundations in NeuroLeadership certification program by NeuroLeadership Institute in Spring 2018.

17. Randy L. Buckner and Daniel C. Carroll. "Self-Projection and the Brain." *Trends in Cognitive Sciences* 11:2 (2006): 49–57.

18. Michael Wilkinson described this technique in an education workshop at the 2014 annual meeting for the International Association of Facilitators.

19. Catherine J. Norris, Jeff T. Larsen, L. Elizabeth Crawford, and John T. Cacioppo. "Better (or Worse) for Some Than Others: Individual Differences in the Positivity Offset and the Negativity Bias." *Journal of Research in Personality* 45:1 (February 2011): 100–11.

20. Michael Wilkinson used this technique at the 2014 annual meeting for the International Association of Facilitators.

21. Valerie Patrick and Laurie Weingart. "Research-Based Ways Conflict Improves Performance." *Fulcrum Connection LLC.* April 19, 2016. *https://fulcrumconnection.com.*

22. Laurie R. Weingart, Kristin Behfar, Corinne Bendersky, Gergana Todorova, and Karen A. Jehn. "The Directness and Oppositional Intensity of Conflict Expression." *Academy of Management Review* 40:2 (April 2014). *http://doi.org/10.5465/amr.2013.0124.*

CHAPTER 7

1. Insights on strategy are based on interviewing twelve executives at Bayer Corporation known for their strategic thinking followed by personal professional experience in strategy development and implementation.

2. Lead by Influencing class by The PAR Group in 2006.

3. John T. Cacioppo, Stephanie Cacioppo, and Richard E. Petty. "The Neuroscience of Persuasion: A Review with an Emphasis on Issues and Opportunities." *Social Neuroscience* 13:2 (2018 April): 129–72.

4. Dawna Markova and Angie McArthur. *Collaborative Intelligence: Thinking with People Who Think Differently* (New York: Random House, 2015), 107–27.

5. Donella H. Meadows. *Thinking in Systems: A Primer* (London, U.K.: Earthscan, 2009), 145–65.

6. Elliot T. Berkman and David Rock. "AIM: An Integrative Model of Goal Pursuit." *NeuroLeadership Journal* 5 (September 2014): 1–15.

7. Morten T. Hansen. *Great at Work: How Top Performers Do Less, Work Better, and Achieve More* (New York: Simon & Schuster, 2018).

8. "Find an IAF Certified Professional Facilitator." *International Association of Facilitators. https://www.iaf-world.org.*

9. Keith Sawyer. *Zig Zag: The Surprising Path to Greater Creativity* (New York: Jossey-Bass, 2013).

10. Valerie Patrick. "Misconceptions About Facilitation," "The Truth About Facilitation Skills," and "The Benefits of Facilitation." *International Institute for Facilitation and Change. https://english.iifac.org.*

11. Valerie Patrick. "Facilitation Perception to End the Misconception." *Fulcrum Connection LLC. December 8, 2015. https://fulcrumconnection.com.*

INDEX

A

ABC'S. *see* Agendas, Barters, Charters, and Starters/Enders (ABC'S) of team operation
accomplishments inventory, 59–60
action items, 166
ADKAR, 118
advanced meeting design, 202–210
advocating process, 95
aerobic exercise, 25–27
age diversity, 1–2
agenda, 161, 167–169
Agendas, Barters, Charters, and Starters/Enders (ABC'S) of team operation, 158–165
"aha" moment, 137
apathy, team leadership and, 70
Around the World (AtW) generating ideas tactic, 177–178
aversive emotion systems, 37

B

Baby Boomers, 1
bad-mouthing, 17
balance, 16
barriers to goals, 78
barters, 161–162, 170
behaviors for strong/healthy relationships, 23
Benioff, Marc, 138
bias blind spot, 93, 105–106
blind input exercise, 94–95
"born with it" creativity myth, 136–137

brain
    cognitive biases and, 92–93
    emotional well-being and, 37–38
    glymphatic system and, 28
    neural connections in, 33–34
    social well-being and, 16
    stimuli, 176–177
    well-being and function of, 15
budget decreases, adjusting for, 116–118

C

career motive categories, 46–47
"Celebrate What's Right with the World" (Dewitt video), 44–45
Center for Creative Leadership (CCL), 71–72
change management process, 118
character, referent power and, 142
charters, 158–161, 169
coercive power, 140
cognitive biases, 92–93
cognitive empathy, 104–105
cognitive well-being, 33–35
    brain and, 33–34
    creativity and, 34
    nutrition and, 34–35
    personal assessment of, 20–21
Collaborative Intelligence (Markova and MacArthur), 61
collaborators, 4
collective intelligence, 4–5
    self-awareness and, 5
compelling vision, 190

competence, expert power and, 141
competition, team climate and,
    145–146, 148
composition. *see* team composition
confusion, 150
consensus, team operation and, 157
consent agenda, 170–171
Covey, Stephen R., 100
Creative Problem Solving Group,
    134
creativity. *see also* team creativity
    cognitive capacity and, 34
    low tolerance to, 130, 131
    myths, 136–138
critical success factors, 78
curiosity, 84, 138–139

D

decision-making, 93–95
    advocating process, 95
    blind input exercise, 94–95
    value development team process,
        94
default mode network, 34
departure process, team membership,
    121–123
design of meeting. *see* meeting design
desires, 47–48
diet, physical well-being and, 27–28
Dietrich, Arne, 93
disruptive behavior management
    tactics, 182–186
diversity
    age/generation, 1–2
    expertise, 2
    team composition and, 110–114
    team members and, 1–2
    visible, 2
documentation of team meetings,
    166–171
    meeting agenda as, 167–169
    minutes template for, 166–167
Drucker, Peter, 75

E

ego, quiet, 5–6
Eisenhower, Dwight D., 82
emotional contagion, 69–70
emotional empathy, 104
Emotional Intelligence Map, 54–55
emotional well-being, 35–39
    brain and, 37–38
    dimensions of, 36–37
    examples of, 35–36
    gender and, 38
    personal assessment of, 21–22
emotions
    managing, 37
    negative, team leaders and, 68–69
    negative, team members and,
        69–70
    negative, team member's social
        needs and, 87–88
    perceiving, 36
    understanding, 37
    using, 37
enders, 162, 173–174
engagement activities, 177–182
Enneagram Personality Portraits
    Inventory and Profile, 53–54
equal participation, team climate
    and team member, 128
"eureka" creativity myth, 137–138
executive attention network, 34
exercise/fitness, 25–26
expectation, team climate and, 147
expert career motive, 47
expertise diversity, 2
expert power, 140–141
    competence and, 141
extrinsic rewards, 43

F

facilitation practices, 155–156,
    174–175, 212–214
finite verb, 78
fixed mindset, 83

Fujitsu's Macroscope methodology, 118

Fulcrum's Facilitation Assessment, 155–156

G

generation diversity, 1–2

Generation X, 1

Generation Y, 1

Generation Z, 2

glymphatic system, 28

goal hierarchy, meeting design and, 195–196

Goleman, Daniel, 69

go or no-go milestone approach, 118

governance plan, 169–170

Group Genius: The Creative Power of Collaboration (Sawyer), 102

groupthink, team composition and, 99

growth mindset, 83

H

Hackman, J. Richard, 101

Hughes, Mark Alan, 188–189

humility, 138–139

I

identity
  personality assessments and, 50–55
  psychological stress and, 55–56
  teamwork and, 49–58
  value assessments and, 57–58

imagination network, 34

implementation challenge, team operation and, 157–158

implicit stereotypes, 105

inclusion
  cognitive empathy and, 104–105
  diversity and, 106–107
  emotional empathy and, 104
  exclusion thoughts and, 105–106
  inclusivity challenge for, 107–110

self-interest and, 103–104
team composition and, 103–110

inclusivity challenge, 107–110

infinite verb, 77

Inklings, The, 137

insights, 137–138

intangible well-being, 29–33
  described, 30
  development of, 31–32
  example of, 29–31
  mindfulness meditation and, 32
  personal assessment of, 19–20
  spiritual practices and, 32
  STPEs and, 31–32

International Association of Facilitators, 157

intrinsic motivation, 148

intrinsic rewards, 43

introvert moment, 178–179

inward focus, 138

irrational behavior, team composition and, 99–100

J

Jones, Dewitt, 44–45, 48, 49

K

Karlgaard, Rich, 102

Kaufman, Scott Barry, 34

Kotter eight-step process for leading change, 118

L

ladder of abstraction, 151

leadership. *see* team leadership challenges; team leaders/leadership

leadership vision principles, 194–195

level setting tactic, 178–179

Lewis, C. S., 137

Lincoln, Abraham, 84

linear career motive, 46

"lone inventor" creativity myth, 137

M

Malone, Michael, 102
managing emotions, 37
MAPP. *see* Motivated Appraisal of
 Personal Potential (MAPP)
 assessment
Markova, Dawna, 61
McArthur, Angie, 61
meeting agenda, 167–169
meeting design, 187–218
 advanced, 202–210
 commitment by team members
  and, 191
 components of, 198–202
 comprehensive inquiry and,
  216–217
 expertise/knowledge/perspectives,
  accessing, 197
 facilitation matrix, 211–214
 goal hierarchy and, 195–196
 information integration and,
  217–218
 leadership vision and, 194–195
 mastering system for, 210–218
 meeting outcomes and, 199–202
 meeting purpose/objectives/
  outcomes, defining, 214–216
 overview of, 187–191
 persuasion and, 191–193
 principles, 194–198
 problems, symptoms of, 191–193
 process leadership/expertise and,
  198
 and strategic context, 190
 vs. team operation, 189
 value maximized and, 196–197
meeting objectives, 162–164
 defining, 214–216
meeting outcomes, 164, 199–202
 defining, 214–216
meeting process operational tactics,
  165–175
 documentation, 166–171

 enders, 173–174
 facilitator, working with,
  174–175
 overview of, 165–166
 starters, 171–173
Millennials, 1
Miller, George, 102
mindfulness meditation, intangible
 well-being and, 32
Mind Manager, 61
mindsets, team leader, 80–85
minority majority, 2
minutes template, 166–167
Motivated Appraisal of Personal
 Potential (MAPP) assessment,
 60
motivation
 for goal pursuit, 79, 148
 Theory of Mind (ToM) and,
  64–65
 workplace, 43
Myers-Briggs Type Indicator
 (MBTI), 50, 52–53

N

National Sleep Foundation, 28–29
negative emotions
 team leaders and, 68–69
 team members and, 69–70
 team member's social needs and,
  87–88
networking profile self-assessment,
 60
NeuroLeadership Institute, 108
Newton, Thandie, 107
nonproductive conflict, 129, 131
nutrition, cognitive well-being and,
 34–35

O

onboarding process, team
 membership, 123–124
out-group bias, 104–105

P

parking lot items, 166, 183
passive-aggressive behavior, 129–130
perceiving emotions, 36
performance-arousal curve, 69
personality assessments, 50–55
personal mastery, 48–49
personal strengths
    accomplishments inventory of,
        59–60
    MAPP assessment of, 60
    networking profile self-assessment
        of, 60
    Reflected Best Self exercise for,
        61
    teamwork and, 58–62
    thinking talents exercise, 61
Personal Values Assessment (PVA),
    57
persuasion, lack of commitment and,
    191–193
physical well-being, 24–29
    in college, 24–25
    diet and, 27–28
    exercise/fitness and, 25–27
    personal assessment of, 19
    sleep and, 28–29
    weight training and, 27
Pink, Daniel, 45
poor planning, team operation and,
    156–157
poor progress, team composition
    and, 100
popularity *vs.* social well-being, 24
positional power, 140
power
    described, 139
    forms of, 140–141
    team climate and, 139–141
principles
    defined, 194
    expertise/knowledge/perspectives,
        accessing, 197

goal hierarchy, 195–196
    leadership vision, 194–195
    of meeting design, 194–198
    process leadership and expertise,
        198
    value maximized, 196–197
prioritizing tactic, 178
productive team conflict, 183
proposed project planning (P3)
    tactic, 179–180
psychological stress, 55–56
purpose, sense of, 43–44
    self-discovery and, 45–47
    statement, 48–49
    teamwork and, 44–49

Q

questioning, 150
quiet ego, 5–6

R

RACI. *see* Responsible, Accountable,
    Consult, and Inform (RACI)
    analysis
Reading-the-Mind-in-the-Eyes score,
    62
referent power, 140–141
    character and, 142
Reflected Best Self exercise, 61
relationships
    behaviors for strong/healthy, 23
    for social well-being, 17, 23–24
Responsible, Accountable, Consult,
    and Inform (RACI) analysis,
    112–113
reward-based curiosity, 84
rewarding emotion systems, 37–38
reward power, 140
roamer career motive, 47

S

salience network, 34
Sawyer, Keith, 102, 137

self-awareness
    collective intelligence and, 5
    teamwork and, 41–44, 61–62
self-discovery, 45–47
self-interest, inclusion and, 103–104
self-transcendent positive emotions
    (STPEs), 31–32
Senge, Peter, 48
sense of purpose, 43–44
    self-discovery and, 45–47
    statement, 48–49
    teamwork and, 44–49
shin splints, 27
situational humility, 81
Situational Outlook Questionnaire,
    134
sleep, physical well-being and,
    28–29
SMART goals, 77–78
social fitness, 24
social intelligence, 12
social needs, team members', 86–92
    approaches to address, 87
social skills, 3–4, 7–8
social well-being, 16–18, 23–24
    health risks from, 16–17
    importance of, 16–17
    personal assessment of, 18
    vs. popularity, 24
    relationships needed for, 17,
      23–24
SOS assessment of team climate, 133
SPICE assessment, 15–16, 39
    of cognitive well-being, 20–21
    of emotional well-being, 21–22
    of intangible well-being, 19–20
    of physical well-being, 19
    of social well-being, 18
spiral career motive, 47
spiritual practices, intangible well-
    being and, 32
stakeholders, 79–80
starters, 162, 171–173

status updates, team process for,
    115–116
stimuli types, 176–177
STPEs. *see* self-transcendent positive
    emotions (STPEs)
strengths. *see* personal strengths
sustainability, 16
Sweet, Julie, 105–106

T

taking action tactic, 179–180
team building, 131
team climate, 127–152
    competition and, 145–146, 148
    components of, 127
    defined, 127
    expectation and, 147
    health check, 132–133
    leadership dynamics impacting,
      139–148
    power and, 139–141
    problems, identifying, 132–136
    problems, symptoms of, 128–132
    SOS assessment of, 133
    team creativity and, 136–139
    team leader influence on, 128
    team member participation and,
      128
    team member role in, 148–152
team climate problems
    identifying, 132–136
    low tolerance to creativity as, 130,
      131
    nonproductive conflict as, 129,
      131
    passive-aggressive behavior as,
      129–130
    symptoms of, 128–132
    team building as, 131
team composition, 97–125
    budget decreases and, 116–118
    change management process and,
      118

diversity and, 110–114
external influences on, 114–120
groupthink and, 99
inclusion and, 103–110
irrational behavior and, 99–100
overview of, 97–99
poor progress and, 100
problems, symptoms of, 99–103
status updates and, 115–116
strategic selection of, 100–103
team membership problems and,
 120–124
team size and, 100–102
team creativity
 assessments, 133–136
 challenges, 136–139
 improving, 134–135
team goals, group process to
 improve, 77–80
team leader mindsets, 80–85
team leadership challenges
 internal, addressing, 75–86
 mindsets, 80–85
 team goals, group process to
  improve, 77–80
 team member one-on-one
  feedback, 85–86
 types of, 71–75
team leaders/leadership
 challenges (*see* team leadership
  challenges)
 described, 67–68
 impacting team climate, 139–148
 mindsets, 80–85
 problems, symptoms of, 68–71
 team member's social needs and,
  86–92
 thinking traps, avoiding, 92–96
team members
 commitment by, meeting design
  and, 191
 participation, team climate and,
  128

team climate role of, 148–152
team operation participation
 tactics, 175–182
unequal participation, team
 operation and, 157
team membership problem fixing,
 120–124
 appreciation for departing
  members and, 122–123
 departure process and, 121–123
 onboarding process and, 123–124
 overview of, 120–121
team operation, 153–186
 ABC'S of, 158–165
 consensus and, 157
 disruption management tactics,
  182–186
 facilitation and, 155–156
 implementation challenges and,
  157–158
 vs. meeting design, 189
 meeting process tactics, 165–175
 overview of, 153–155
 poor planning and, 156–157
 problem types, 155–158
 team member participation
  tactics, 175–182
 unequal member participation
  and, 157
team performance self-assessment,
 142–145
teamwork
 collaborators and, 4
 diversity and, 1–2
 generations of employees and, 1–2
 identity and, 49–58
 introduction to, 1–5
 mastering, reasons for, 6–7
 measuring performance of, 4–5
 need for, 3–4
 personal strengths and, 58–62
 self-awareness and, 41–44
 self-discovery and, 45–47

sense of purpose and, 44–49
skills needed for, 3–4, 7–8
Theory of Mind (ToM) and,
     62–65
and well-being (*see* well-being)
Theory of Mind (ToM)
   described, 62
   motivation and, 64–65
   teamwork and, 62–65
thinking talents exercise, 61
thinking traps
   decision-making and, 93–95
   defined, 92
   team leadership, avoiding, 92–96
thoughtful tactics, 85–86
Tolkien, J. R. R., 137
Traditionalists, 1
trust, 110–111
trust building tactic, 180–181

U
understanding building tactic,
     181–182
understanding emotions, 37
unproductive team conflict, 183
   managing, 183–184
using emotions, 37

V
value assessments, 57–58
value development team process, 94
value maximized principles, 196–197
Vidmar, Neil, 101
visible diversity, 2

W
weight training, 27
well-being, 11–39. *see also* individual
     dimensions of
   brain function and, 15
   cognitive, 33–35
   dimensions of, 15–16
   emotional, 35–39
   for first-time moms, 14–15
   intangible, 29–33
   overview of, 11–16
   physical, 24–29
   social, 16–18, 23–24
   work-family experience with,
      12–14
white male minority, 2
Winfrey, Oprah, 45
workplace motivation, 43

ABOUT THE AUTHOR

Dr. Valerie Patrick, President of Fulcrum Connection LLC, is a facilitator, leadership trainer, and speaker who has helped a wide variety of technical organizations improve performance through science-based leadership and collaboration since 2014. Dr. Patrick is a PhD chemical engineer with twenty-five years of corporate experience leading technical and strategic initiatives to identify and deliver new sources of organizational value at Bayer and Monsanto. Her last corporate position was serving four years as the first Sustainability Coordinator and Strategist for Bayer North America (BNA) reporting to CEO Greg Babe. In that role, she launched BNA's first sustainability report, BNA's first GHG emission reduction commitment, and an employee sustainability thinking education program that reduced environmental impacts while generating millions of dollars in business benefits.

Dr. Patrick was one of three women in her college class of twenty-four chemical engineers at Bucknell University, and she was one of two women in her graduate school class of sixteen at the California Institute of Technology.

Dr. Patrick wasn't aware of the performance barriers associated with gender diversity until she was promoted to her first corporate management job in 1994. In this position, she was the only female research manager reporting to a male director of research along with five other male research managers. Her ability to interact effectively and contribute in male majority situations was recognized by a vice president who invited her to participate in his staff meetings as a developmental assignment.

Dr. Patrick has more than 10,000 hours of corporate experience as a team leader, another 10,000 hours of experience as a Certified Professional Facilitator (obtained through the International Association of Facilitators), is a Certified Creative Problem Solving Facilitator through the Creative Problem Solving Group, and is certified with distinction in the Foundations of NeuroLeadership by the NeuroLeadership Institute.